In my last meeting with Taiichi Ohno, he gave me calligraphies for "Challenge" and "Beyond the Conventional Belief." Living out his terms is a way of "Awakening." I hope Dan's book will help readers find such a moment and benefit many.

Kiyoshi Suzaki, author of The New Shop Floor Management *and* Results with a Heart

Wow! In this great book, you will benefit from a clear understanding of Lean thinking, leadership, and states of being. It's like hanging out after work, a nice combination of compelling stories, deep learning, Zen and the Sensei Way.

Kevin Coray, Ph.D., Extraordinary Teams Partnership

Lean managers are entrusted to both "Get the work done and develop your people." Ambidexterity is required. But just how many ambidextrous pitchers have you known?

John Shook, author of Managing to Learn, *Chairman the Lean Global Network and Senior Advisor, Lean Enterprise Institute*

In *The Sensei Way at Work*, Dan shares a fresh perspective and a treasure of historical anecdotes, vivid teaching that enables the reader to grasp the value and practice of the Lean Sensei.

Michael Orzen, co-author of the Shingo Prize-winning book Lean IT

It has been 25 years since *Lean Thinking* was published, and many enterprises are struggling to create a work culture like Toyota's. Is there a secret Toyota hasn't shared? There isn't one. Problem is, to the western management mind, the critical element simply isn't recognizable. It's executives and managers with Kaizen Mind who lead, teach, and coach continuous improvement. In *The Sensei Way at Work*, Dan Prock provides a detailed guide to the ways of being, thinking, practices, and skills that leaders must develop both in themselves and in employees that make continuous improvement a way of doing business. Creating a culture of continuous improvement can't be delegated. It has to be led, and this book gives an engaging and enlightening description of how to and by whom.

David Verble, a former Human Resource Development Manager, problem solving teacher, and coach at North American Toyota, and currently a Partner in the Lean Transformations Group

The Sensei Way at Work isn't just another spin on "lean." It offers great insight on why something so conceptually simple is so challenging to sustain. The challenge is developing leaders with a low-ego, observant, ongoing curiosity, and who become sensei for others.

Robert W. "Doc" Hall, a founding member of the Association for Manufacturing Excellence, judge for IndustryWeek Magazine's *Best Plants Program, and currently Chairman, Compression Institute*

The Sensei Way at Work

The Sensei Way at Work
The Five Keys to a Lean
Business Transformation

Dan Prock
Foreword by John Shook

A PRODUCTIVITY PRESS BOOK

First published 2021
by Routledge
600 Broken Sound Parkway #300, Boca Raton FL, 33487

and by Routledge
2 Park Square, Milton Park, Abingdon, Oxon, OX14 4RN

Routledge is an imprint of the Taylor & Francis Group, an informa business

ISBN: 9780367376147 (hbk)
ISBN: 9780367370701 (pbk)
ISBN: 9780429355271 (ebk)

Typeset in Garamond
by codeMantra

DEDICATION

I am a belonger in a world of infinite possibilities, where happiness is the earned reward of caring.

Remembering My Days, by Grandmother Lalla Prock

Contents

Foreword

The Questions

How is a factory like a motorcycle?
How is throwing a baseball like a Zen stick?
How is being a sensei like fixing a motorcycle?
If you find these questions compelling, this book is for you. And you've found the right guide in author Dan Prock.

The Challenge

Dan is a former baseball pitcher, engineer, student of Zen meditation and Western psychology, a lean consultant, and an executive coach for the Toyota Way. In our first conversation in 2013, he made a statement in a manner that was both matter-of-fact and bold: "Sakichi Toyoda was a Buddhist engineer, I know because I'm a Buddhist engineer, and I'm going to write a book about it." I was taken aback. "How presumptuous," I thought, "making claims to know the mind of Sakichi (inventor and founder of the Toyota group who lived from 1867 to 1930), who died almost a century ago!" Later I learned that Dan had been both a Zen student and a fastball pitcher, and he wasn't afraid to throw under your chin to make a point. Chin music meets Zen stick thwap! Dan's words served their intended purpose and got my attention.

Sakichi Toyoda was indeed a Buddhist. Yet the religious affiliation of the founder of the Toyota group of companies is not the usual fodder of books about lean transformation. So, you may rightly ask, what does that have to do with achieving a lean business transformation? The answer can be found in *The Sensei Way at Work*.

Lean thinking enables improving work systems or transforming an organization, which in turn entails improving capabilities – the technologies employed in an operation and the thinking and skills of the humans who comprise it. Since the beginning of organization improvement as a formal discipline in the early decades of the 20th century, the question of how to transform an organization and impart new knowledge and skills to employees has steadily garnered increased interest. Cottage industries have cropped up: organizational development, business transformation consulting, and skills training and education. Now, in the early years of the 21st century, executive coaching has emerged as a core discipline to enable organizational change.

In fact, in lean organizations, managers are compelled to develop coaching skills in order to not only achieve results but also elevate the capabilities of their people. Lean managers are entrusted to both "Get the work done and develop your people." No less an authority than Sakichi's great grandson (and CEO of Toyota today) Akio Toyoda states unequivocally, "We say at Toyota that every leader is a teacher developing the next generation of leaders. This is their most important job." But few mortal managers are equally equipped to accomplish both tasks. In fact, managers who excel at one are usually frightfully deficient in the other. Ambidexterity is required. But just how many ambidextrous pitchers have you known?

Enter the Sensei

Since sensei is just a word, we humans can define it however we wish. It is often used as just another word for teacher or coach. Dan has a definition in mind, which he will share with you. For now, the word itself begs some exploration into its Japanese roots. Many Japanese terms have been introduced to the English-speaking business world and many of them take on a life of their own, straying far from their original meaning in Japanese.

According to most popular Japanese–English dictionaries, sensei simply means "teacher." In Japanese, it's a compound word – composed of the two kanji or Chinese characters 先 (sen) and 生 (sei) – meaning "one who was born before," or "one who has gone before," or "one who teaches on the basis of experience or age." Medical doctors are commonly referred to as sensei, and sometimes simply being old is enough to be called sensei. Beyond that, it means "one who has gone before," and entails sensei who engages in the direct transmission of knowledge or skill to a leader – that is, one accomplished "mind to mind."

Usage of the term sensei in LeanWorld is not particularly unique, but it does have its specific connotations especially in connection with the founder of Toyota Production System (TPS) Taiichi Ohno, his band of direct disciples (notably Kikuo Suzumura and Fujio Cho, but many more, both inside and outside Toyota), and the thousands who have received transmission from them.

Importantly, as with many key Japanese concepts, the term sensei implies a relationship. In the case of sensei, there is a relationship between the "teacher" and the "learner" that invokes the connotation of "master" and perhaps "apprentice." When Ohno's disciples refer to "Ohno Sensei," they use the term with deep respect for their teacher and in reverence of their relationship with him. Different terms can be used, but a common one in this context is deshi (弟子, another compound word). In domains that require many years of deep study or practice, there is no sensei (teacher) without a deshi or someone being taught. Thus, the sensei is one part of a dyad that includes, of equal importance, a learner. (One can easily imagine how the famous slogan – "If the learner hasn't learned, the teacher hasn't taught" – of the American Training Within Industry program had such immediate resonance when it was introduced to Japanese ears in the late 1940s!)

Once formed, sensei–deshi relationships typically last a lifetime, entailing obligations on each side. Neither side quits unless the other betrays or fails to hold up his/her end of the mutual obligations. Former Toyota Chairman Fujio Cho was a direct deshi of Taiichi Ohno and is a sensei for Akio Toyoda. This important dimension is usually missing in the Western (LeanWorld or other) usage of the term. (To learn more of the deeper cultural dimensions of the term sensei, read the novel Kokoro – kokoro means "heart" or "the heart of things" or "heart-mind." The original title in Japanese was something like Kokoro – A Sensei's Testament – by Natsume Soseki.)

Considering the complexity of the term sensei underscores a deeply held doubt regarding language that is shared between Buddhists and Toyota lean sensei: they both distrust language implicitly. Those curious Zen koan you've heard about? As much as anything, they are intended to clear the mind of the false dichotomies that are present whenever we define things. For example, a motorcycle is not a car. Clearly. On the other hand, they are both vehicles to move around people or goods. Does two wheels versus three matter? There are cars with three wheels, and there are motorcycles with three wheels. If you try to answer a koan with a Kierkegaardian yes–no, the sensei's response will likely be a crisp thwap with the Zen stick. The teacher's intent is to clear your mind of either–or dichotomies in order to enable you to see things as they are, as part of a whole, each thing in harmony with all the others. You can't even have yes without no.

"Name it and you kill it" were the words of Taiichi Ohno (so I am told) when his team insisted on naming the system of work organization that has become known as the TPS. Prior to that time, the system of concepts and techniques including Just-in-Time, pull, Kanban, Jidoka, poka-yoke, and so many more were known either as "the Ohno system" or "the Toyota system" or "the Kanban system" or "JIT" or nothing. Ohno would have preferred it remain nothing. TPS isn't a "thing" so much as a way of thinking to get things done.

A Process? A Way to Think? A Way to Be?

Most modern definitions of "coaching" in a business context (there are many kinds of coaches) draw a distinct line which the coach mustn't cross between concern for the process and concern for the result. Coaches coach only the process, concerning themselves little or not at all with the actual task at hand, which is up to the learner, who is, after all, the "expert" who must "own" the outcome.

Indeed, that any result is the result of a process is a core belief of lean thinking. If you want a better result, focus on changing the process. And, indeed, ownership of the outcome must remain with the learner. And which is it that matters – the outcome or the process? Ask that question and expect some chin music from Dan the pitcher, or a Zen stick thwap! from the author.

Yes, focus on the process. Improve the process and the result will follow. Kaizen, kaizen, kaizen. But how do you know if you're making progress? How do you know if the changes you are making on your process are "right" or are progressing you toward your goal? Here's how to address that question in a way that is opposite the philosophy of most executive coaching models: Whether you call yourself coach or sensei or teacher or consultant – did your learner improve the work? Was quality made better? Did you take some "muri" (overburden) off the workers back? Did you alleviate some struggle? Was some cost eliminated to provide better value for the customer? Did the motorcycle start?

The 1974 book *Zen and the Art of Motorcycle Maintenance* by Robert Pirsig introduced many Westerners to an interpretation of Zen Buddhism. The book wasn't much about Zen, really, but the Zen idea expressed in the book is that the best teacher for an apprentice motorcycle mechanic is an inoperative motorcycle. The apprentice can apply every tool in the shop, but his/her efforts and learning will come down to one ultimate thing: whether the damned thing starts. If it starts, okay, perhaps you learned something; move on to the next. If it didn't start, step back, clear the mind, focus on the problem, access your accumulated learning (sorry if what comes next sounds like pop Zen from a Keanu Reeves movie), and let your way of being become one with the task at hand. Just try. Try, reflect, learn. Improve the work. Any good baseball pitcher comes to grips with this idea of being. (If you want more on sports and Zen, try the book that was Mr. Pirsig's inspiration, *Zen and the Art of Archery*, which was written by a German living in pre-Second World War Japan. You'll never read more profound expression of "mind the process, shoot the arrow, throw the pitch…just mind the process.")

What Then, Does the Sensei Own?

Which brings us back to the factory as a motorcycle and how it relates to what Dan calls the Sensei Way. Before my experience working for Toyota in 1980s Japan, I was on the receiving end of many thwaps from the Zen stick delivered by my many sensei at Eiheiji, the Zen temple founded in the 13th century by Zen master Dogen.

It was in order to learn more that I decided to next seek work at the most culturally Japanese company I could find. I felt certain that the spirit of Zen was still alive in Japan, not in temples or in martial arts classes, but hidden just beneath the surface in the teeming life of Japanese corporations. I was right, and I was wrong. I had presumed all Japanese companies were the same, a misconception, which is far, far from the truth.

In *The Training of the Zen Buddhist Monk*, D. T. Suzuki argues, "Zen is a discipline, not a religion." At Toyota, I found Zen practiced in the dogged focus and the discipline of minding the mundane; the sensei's ethos rang through my being as I received job instructions that enabled me to perform quality work safely and efficiently as I climbed in and out of a Corolla 500 times a day. The TPS now has a name, but naming it hasn't killed it. And even today, motorcycle mechanics are still learning in the same centuries-old way.

John Shook
Ann Arbor, Michigan

Acknowledgments

Thanks go to a number of people who helped me on my quest to learn the Sensei Way. First thanks go to my best baseball coaches Leo Hesse, Elmer Weishman, and Steve Schafbuch. Noteworthy instructors at the University of Utah include Frederick Herzberg, Martin Chemers, and Oakley Gordon, and at the Gestalt Institute of Cleveland, thanks go to Carolyn Lukensmeyer. Thanks for the interviews for this book from authors Art Byrne, Robert "Doc" Hall, Jeffrey Liker, and Mike Rother, and special appreciation goes to John Shook for his encouragement to write it. Thanks for the contributions and role modeling of fellow change leaders, consultants, and coaches including Katrina Appell, Gary Bergmiller, Beth Carrington, John Drogosz, Joe Duffy, Charles Ellenbecker, Thomas Hartman, Mike Ward, Cyd Henrikson, Howard Kinkade, Derek Kotze, Bob Kucner, Ron Lumsden, Michael Funke, Frank Gianattassio, Chad Moore, Mike Orzen, Ron Oslin, Sarah Patterson, James Rollo, David Verble, and James Van Patton. Credits to Pat Panchak for the editorial advice, and Vicki Rollo for the graphics. Special thanks to my compatriot and Zen sage, Tom Lane. Great love and thanks to my daughter Stevie and infinite love to my father Gene Doil Prock.

Author

Dan Prock grew up pitching a baseball and learned the inner state of being that enables high performance. After he received a degree in engineering, he worked several years as a quality engineer in construction. Later, after two advanced degrees in psychology, he was hired and promoted to a director at Cummins Engine Company, where he learned about systems thinking and the Toyota Production System. He attended the organization and systems development program at the Gestalt Institute of Cleveland and sat in meditation at the Zen Center of San Francisco and the Shambhala Meditation Center in Colorado, and at many other centers. He has been associated with the Kaizen Institute of America, Optiprise Consulting, Competitive Advantage Consultants, the Association for Manufacturing Excellence, and the Lean Enterprise Institute.

Prologue: Playing in the Zone

At seven o'clock on a hot summer night in Wichita, I was the starting pitcher against the McConnell team in the Victory league. During my warm-up, I had found a rhythm, let go to the idea of winning or losing, become present and entered the state of flow. All signs were that it would not be a good night for my opponents. Fast forward through eight scoreless innings, my team leads 1–0, and the best hitter in the league stepped up for a final at bat. After three straight strikeouts, Josh was surely determined to redeem himself with a hit or at least a hard-hit ball somewhere. As he stepped into the batter's box, our eyes met briefly. I felt neither pride nor sympathy about Josh's tough night. Those are emotions that arise from ego, and I was pitching in the zone, a state of being where ego cannot go.

A 95 mile-per-hour fast ball takes four-tenths of a second to reach the hitting zone, that's 400 milliseconds. The hitter has only the first 250 milliseconds to see the pitcher's release point, get an image of the ball's spin, estimate its trajectory and velocity, and make a decision to swing in a way that puts the barrel of the bat in contact on the center of gravity of the baseball. If a hitter isn't fully present, a fastball seems to dart faster than his eyes can follow and a curveball dives down toward the earth faster than a hitter can anticipate and hit.

Unfortunately for pitchers, a metaphysical thing happens to a hitter when he or she finds the zone. Time slows. In the zone, a hitter's sense of time bears little relation to the absolute passage of time on a clock. There, a hitter's perception becomes dense, slowing his experience of time. In that state, a fast pitch seems slower, the ball appears bigger, and its spin is readily read. A hitter "locked in" to the zone tracks a pitch with a perceptial radar that's wired directly to muscle memory. Hitters in the zone are not nice to pitchers.

Just staying mindful and observing Josh, I noticed that in this at bat he was standing very near home plate. It's a more aggressive hitting position, and by standing close, he indicated he was expecting an "away" pitch location, perhaps like the side-armed curve that I'd struck him out with earlier. I considered a brush-back pitch, a little "chin music" to set up another sidewinder on the fourth pitch. But an arising insight told me to crowd him with a fastball inside near his belt buckle. It would be a risky pitch because he might be able "turn on it," that is, pull it hard to left field, and maybe even hit a homer and tie the game. That's why he wouldn't expect it.

Following my insight, I threw the inside fastball, and as he began to swing at the sweet pitch, he stopped himself and took it. The umpire called "strike one." Josh's natural reflexes had signaled him to swing, but an expectation blocked his natural ability. Another fixed thought would soon lead to his final defeat. On the second pitch, he was unable to track the sharp downward arc of the knuckle curve, and he swung through a layer of air above it for strike two. The best hitter in the league was now only one strike away from a 0-for-4 night.

All strikeouts.

Now it's normal for a pitcher with a two-strike, no ball count on a hitter to waste a pitch. It's a no-lose tactic because an anxious hitter may swing at a pitch way outside, too high or down and in the dirt. Of course, good hitters know this protocol and usually resist a tempting pitch outside the strike zone. I paused and asked myself what were the chances that the best hitter in the league would take a foolish swing? I let go of all thoughts and entered into the state of presence and time became dense. Once there, a lucid awareness told me he was alternately blinking and staring me down. Moments later, his eye-blinking slowed and he appeared more relaxed. Then, the next intuition arrived. Josh was expecting me to follow the "waste one" rule, and aiming to amp up and hit the fourth pitch a few moments later.

But there wouldn't be a fourth pitch.

Josh was betting in a world of percentages, yet high performers know that for any single play a percentage may not hold. Staying present and relying on intuition gave me an advantage over Josh's belief in the existence of an objective truth in baseball reality. So, riding a surge of creative energy and absolute certainty that he would let the pitch pass by, and so much joy inside that I had to hold back a laugh, I threw a full-velocity fastball right over the heart of home plate. At a different pitch count, Josh might well have been ready and crushed it. Yet blinded by an idea, he never saw it coming. He wasn't fully present in the moment. Josh struck out looking, paralyzed by a thought in his mechanistic mind. Called out, he stood for a moment in denial, looking down where a perfect pitch had just passed by untouched. He blinked his eyes once, then twice as he absorbed the meaning of the umpire's final two words of the night.

What part of "strike three" didn't he understand?

Yet Josh was a pro and he knew that this was only one game. He looked up from the plate and gave me a slight head nod, tipping his cap, but surely meaning, "You won tonight rookie, but it will be different next time." I appreciated his classy gesture. Then he dropped his tar-covered bat in the hot Kansas dust and disappeared into the dark Wichita night. It was a moment after 10 PM.

Back in my pitching days, I discovered that the only meaningful goal was to find the zone and play there as long as possible.[1] It's a divine feeling. I still miss it to this day. Once my playing days were over, I began a quest to find it in the world of work.

---

[1] References to playing in the zone are frequently cited in print from many sports stars. One is from New York Times, On Tennis, Novak Djokovic in *Djokovic and Nadal Are Set for Another Epic Duel Down Under,* By Kurt Streeter, January 25, 2019.

Introduction

Three threads from my work and life combined to weave the fabric of *The Sensei Way at Work*. The first thread was the book *How Things Work*, which my father gave me for Christmas when I was about eight years old. It explained the operations of commonplace machines, ranging from flushing toilets to burning rocket motors. Thereafter, from my first bike ride through my time as an engineer, and on to lean consulting and executive coaching, I've been motivated to figure out how people and systems together can do their best work, and ultimately how transformational business change leaders can be developed.

I discovered the second thread when I sat in meditation one Saturday morning on the floor at a college book store. There, and in numerous meditation halls over the years, I learned to be mindful of continuous changing situations and to be present with people, even when facing uncertainty or conflict.

The revelation of the third thread was the result of playing baseball over the years. As a pitcher, I was immersed in the head-to-head competition with hitters and learned that my best performances happened when I could find and play in the zone, a state that psychologists call "flow." The weaving of these three threads, how things work, mindfulness of how things are, and staying present and finding flow during challenges, became the three essentials of my way of working, parenting, and living. I'll use the Enneagram model to map the nine chapters of *The Sensei Way at Work*.

It's a Wabi Sabi World

The Sensei Way 8   9   1 Lost in Translation

Change Leadership 7   2 Ackoff's Mess

Lean Coaching 6   3 Western Business Goes East

Lean Thinking 5   4 Kaizen Mind

In Chapter 1, *Lost in Translation*, I'll describe how the early Japanese sensei in America and Europe showed us Westerners how to continuously improve our work systems, develop employees, and utilize challenges to develop new change leaders. However, the Sensei Way was lost in translation.

In Chapter 2, *Ackoff's Mess*, I'll review how mid-20th-century American factories fell from the "golden age of capitalism" into Ackoff's Mess. Meanwhile, Toyota and a few sister companies in Japan adopted an Asian leadership philosophy and a practice of continuous improvement that led a new kind of production system and success.

In Chapter 3, *Western Business Goes East*, I'll describe my interviews with Western executives, plant managers, and experts who benchmarked Toyota's production system in the late 20th century. Yet, while Western managers could start Toyota-style lean production back home, their organizations couldn't sustain its initial potential. This chapter introduces the five keys to a lean business transformation.

In Chapter 4, *The First Key Is Kaizen Mind*, I'll define kaizen the way author Masaaki Imai did: "Small improvements, involving everyone, that don't cost a lot of money." However, while lots of kaizen can clean up Ackoff's Mess, it doesn't often align improvements in a lean value stream that accumulates a greater value all the way to customers.

In Chapter 5, *The Second Key Is Lean Thinking*, I'll describe how 21st-century Western change leaders are using lean thinking in many types of business to envision a future-state operations in order to prioritize and align kaizen ideas and systems improvements. However, when impatient managers or experts rush to apply value stream mapping and lean work methods, very few employees are motivated to sustain them, at least, not for long.

In Chapter 6, *The Third Key Is Lean Coaching*, I'll describe the three disciplined practices of lean coaching. It has proven effective in engaging employees in continuous improvement, often in a work center. However, when powerful business or site managers hold discordant visions or opposing leadership philosophies, their unresolved conflict is pushed down and middle managers often neglect or disrupt lean coaches' efforts to start and sustain lean work centers and link up product value streams.

In Chapter 7, *The Fourth Key Is Change Leadership*, I'll describe my research on the work of and the mind of a change leader. Yet who can develop the mind of a leader in Western managers?

In Chapter 8, *The Fifth Key Is the Sensei Way*, I'll describe the four stages a sensei uses to mentor a new, aspiring change leader. The sensei elevates the consciousness of an aspiring leader by repeatedly throwing her into Zen experience and may strike with the Zen stick.

In Chapter 9, *It's a Wabi Sabi World*, I'll describe the dramatic conclusion of the story of the Tennessee auto-parts plant. After my final day on its shop floor, I experienced a personal revelation.

In the Epilogue, *Be the Change*, I'll describe my consulting assignment immediately following the Tennessee plant. It's a case that illustrates that despite years of experience and like most everyone, when I faced uncertainty and potential conflict, I once again had to realize and do the one big thing.

Chapter 1

Lost in Translation

The sensei means highly respected teacher. The sensei is not there to be the technical expert making design decisions or the architect of the transformation but rather to work through others by teaching and guiding them.[1]

Jeffrey K. Liker

Zen is so thoroughly integrated into the Japanese psyche that its influence is apparent in every aspect of the life of the people of modern Japan.[2]

Roger J. Davies

IN THE TENNESSEE PLANT

On my first day of a new consulting assignment, I stood atop a stairway overlooking the Tennessee plant's 420,000 square foot shop floor and some 400 hundred employees, except for the 20 percent or so who didn't show up on any given day. Seeing it all, I silently asked myself: I wonder what the heck goes on in here? My answer was: I have no idea. However, as a saying goes, if you really want to understand something, try to change it. Sure enough, as new leaders arrived and a continuous improvement program progressed, I would learn a lot about the plant's work, its problems, its culture, and about the new paradigm of leadership required to transform a traditional Western factory into a Toyota-style lean operation.

The Tennessee auto-parts plant's lean transformation was led by two successive plant managers, a former union president, a Japanese sensei, along with his cadre of American lean consultants, and was supported by a committed vice president who set the direction and paid the bills. After a few years, the plant's once-disengaged workforce, one that corporate staffers had privately derided as a bunch of "shade tree mechanics," had become motivated to learn and able to operate a world-class factory.

What's the Problem to Solve?

Western executives, plant managers, and value stream managers have spent three decades and untold resources trying to start and sustain Toyota-style lean production in their business operations. Yet despite small-scale successes, the consensus of leaders, authors, and lean experts is that after an initial burst of enthusiasm, less than 10 percent of lean value stream startups sustain their initial promise.

Why so?

Due to minimal staffing, synchronized timing, reliance on technical departments, and frequent delivery of information or small lots of components from parallel functions or suppliers, sustaining a lean value stream requires near 100 percent engagement from employees, so that when quality problems or process anomalies arise, they respond quickly or call for support. The problem is, in a recent series of Gallup surveys,[3] some two-thirds of responding employees reported that they were either "disengaged" or "highly disengaged" in their work. So while those disengaged will try lean work methods in order keep their jobs, not many are willing to sustain the discipline required to sustain a lean value stream long term. And it's broadly acknowledged that most middle managers and supervisors consider all improvement programs, including Toyota-style lean operations, as just management's "flavors of the month." So the problem to solve in sustaining lean startups is teaching Western managers a new way of leading, one that gets most everyone engaged. That means, rather than using the force of authority or the authority of expertise, managers must learn a way to engage employees that motivates them to continuously improve the work itself and their own skills. And then a second problem remains: Who will be able to develop these new change leaders? The early Japanese sensei working in American and European factories made leading change look easy. They knew how to develop change leaders because they had been developed the same way by their own sensei years before. In week-long kaizen events, they set direction toward an ideal "waste-free" operation and motivated us Westerners with a special power, one that's still a mystery to most in the West. Those early Japanese sensei flew across big oceans and showed us the way to turn the five keys to a lean business transformation.

Unfortunately, the Sensei Way was lost in translation.

Notes

1 *The Toyota Way to Continuous Improvement*, James K. Franz, David Meier and Jeffrey K. Liker, McGraw-Hill Professional, 2011, p. 382.
2 *Japanese and American Rhetoric: A Contrastive Study*, G. Claiborne, Doctoral Dissertation, University of South Florida; cited in Japanese Culture, Roger J. Davies, Tuttle Publishing, 2016, p. 89.
3 *Factors Driving Record High Employee Engagement in the US*, Jim Harter, Gallup Workplace, February 4, 2020. www.Gallup.com

Chapter 2

Ackoff's Mess

Every problem interacts with other problems and is therefore part of a set of interrelated problems, a system of problems. I choose to call such a system a mess.[1]

Russell L. Ackoff

When the General is entangled in material things and becomes confused and weak, he loses his authority. Then the soldiers under him do not avail themselves of his knowledge but look to themselves alone, and pursue their private plans. And as each one is working for himself, the camp is in disorder, with riots and affrays, and in the end the army meets a disastrous defeat.[2]

Tengugeijutsu, Chissai

IN THE TENNESSEE PLANT

At nine o'clock one summer morning, the atmosphere inside the Tennessee plant was already hot and stuffy. The building had neither windows nor air conditioning, and by afternoon, the temperature on the shop floor could reach a hundred degrees. The only fresh air came in through the open doors at the loading docks and hot air only exited through a few roof vents.

At break time, workers walked on dirty, oily floors and arrived at a minuscule canteen or at a trashed, filthy bathroom where writing in the stalls cursed company managers. Walking those same aisles, I saw machine operators standing near inches-deep piles of metal shavings called "chips," shards that had flown out from open cutting machines. Droplets of cutting oil flew out too and streamed into the piles of chips, forming a heavy metallic sludge that the operator periodically pushed away with a shovel.

Quality was so bad some days that finished parts had to be sold for scrap metal. Why? At times, old equipment couldn't hold an original equipment manufacturer's modern specifications. At other times, the operator was at fault, sometimes not being mindful of the wear on a cutting insert he might fail to adjust the machine accordingly. On occasion, specifications weren't met because maintenance personnel hadn't performed a scheduled preventative maintenance on a machine. Why not? Most were angry at the plant's human resources manager, who hated the union and as a result had under-staffed the unionized crafts for years. They, in turn, retaliated by taking extra breaks to smoke a cigarette and talk behind the plant, or even share a joint. Cocaine was rumored to be sold back there too, although no charges were ever filed.

When machines broke down, supervisors told employees to stand around until a maintenance man arrived. If he couldn't fix a machine quickly, employees were told to stack off half-finished parts on line-side pallets. The parts might then be finished on the second shift or failing that, be done the following Saturday or Sunday on overtime. After a few years, supervisors' main goal became doing just good enough to get by, to make enough good parts to ship to a customer's assembly plant by Friday and avoid blame from their boss. Some weeks, a production line fell so far behind that a chartered jet flew a single pallet of its parts to Detroit late Sunday-night to fill line-side racks for final assembly on vehicles the next morning.

Walking the floor one day, I spoke to one woman who was using a broomstick to free up jammed parts on a conveyor beyond her reach. After chatting a bit, I asked her: How long have you been using the broomstick? Her answer was: Seven years. Factory supervisors knew that employees didn't often deserve blame for production problems. One likened getting production out every day to straightening a tangled line on the bottom of his Tennessee fishing boat. He shared with me in private that: Employees aren't bad; they're disheartened.

The Tennessee auto-parts plant was built during the economic boom after the Second World War, a unique time now known as "the golden age of capitalism." As soldiers returned home and started families, they bought houses, cars, and consumer goods. The American economy grew at over 4 percent per year during the 1950s and at nearly 5 percent throughout the 1960s. The rapid growth boosted corporate profits, which in turn strengthened the bargaining hand of unions, and they negotiated dramatic gains in pay and benefits. As compensation rose for both managers and union employees, an American middle class grew. It was a time when a rising tide in business raised all boats. Yet there was a downside.

Responding to the boom, corporate executives empowered their marketing managers to maximize revenue, and they in turn pushed division and plant managers to increase production beyond their factory's proven production capacity and quality capability. When equipment failed, tired employees took extra days off, quality defects were found by inspectors, or production stalled and deliveries became late, operations managers, engineers, and supervisors spent their days and into their nights night fire-fighting machine or quality problems. Inevitably, some of the tired and frustrated managers blamed the employees nearest a machine breakdown or a quality issue, and those workers retaliated by fingering support functions or criticizing a supplier, and many became disengaged from their jobs. Some factories became perpetual-motion machines of wasteful production, poor product quality, management blame, and employee disengagement. It was such a common industrial plight that a famous professor of systems management gave it a name.

Ackoff's Mess

When I first read the writings of Dr. Russell Ackoff, I felt that I'd found a kindred spirit. He was a professor emeritus of Management Science at the Wharton School, University of Pennsylvania. Dr. Ackoff was a pioneer in the field of operations research, systems thinking, and management science. He was perhaps the first management expert to drill down and identify that the root problem causing chaotic factory production was the fact that modern corporations had failed to adapt their management approach to a fundamental change in business.

Ackoff's central idea was that business had entered into a system's age, a time when rapid change caused compound, tangled sets of problems, what he christened a "mess." He wrote that the root problem causing the mess was: "The search for simple, if not simple-minded solutions to complex problems is a consequence of the inability to deal effectively with complexity."[3] When operations managers tried to resolve sets of related issues one by one, they spent their time fire-fighting each of them, even while new problems arose. As a result, they often became caught in a never-ending game of "whack a mole."

Dr. Ackoff's contention was that resolving the mess in a typical big operation required resolving sets of problems "as sets." He proposed that companies practice an adaptive management process that he called "idealized design," and he defined the ideal as, "a picture of the system as its designers would build now, if they could replace the current system with whatever they wanted most." Redesigning an operation to better adapt to arising problems and customer changes is what we might these days call an "evergreen future-state vision." Since all important questions in an ideal design couldn't be answered at the start, Ackoff asked managers to do operations experiments that could test alternate facility layouts and methods of doing the work. Dr. Ackoff was way ahead of his time, and while he did find receptive executives in some American corporations,[4] his approach didn't spread widely.

So how did the majority of 20th-century operations managers respond when their operations got caught up in Ackoff's Mess? Most simply doubled down on the traditional paradigm of command-and-control management and continued to fight problems whack-a-mole style. In the 21st century, most have dropped command and control in favor of a philosophy of pragmatism, that is, doing whatever it takes to get results, combined with empiricism, using metrics to identify and attack priority problems one by one. In their book, The Moment of Clarity, coauthors Christian Madsbjerg and Mikel Rasmussen described the management mindset that dominates in the 21st century.[5] If you haven't experienced a number of items on this list, you haven't worked in a big Western enterprise.

- Anything uncertain is a problem.
- Problems are deconstructed into quantifiable and formal problem statements (issues).
- Each problem is atomized into the smallest possible bits that can be analyzed separately.
- A list of hypotheses to explain the causes of the problems is generated.
- Data are gathered and processed to test each hypothesis.
- An analysis is used to test each hypothesis, clarify the problems, and find areas of intervention with the highest impact.
- A well-organized structure is deployed to build a logical fact-based argument and ends with a prioritized list of actions, to which the company should adhere.
- All actions are described as must-win battles for which a responsible committee or person is assigned.
- Proposed metrics and a time frame with follow-up monitoring are put in place to track each committee as they complete each task.
- When all committee work has been completed, the problem is solved.

When pressure rises to resolve a problem quickly, some pragmatic managers will inevitably objectify employees as mere "parts" of a troublesome system and thus fail to respect them or consider their input for solving it. Then, after a work process or quality solution is implemented, yet problems persist or resurface later, management plays a game that's familiar to everyone who has ever had a job.

The Blame Game

The blame game is so familiar to working people that it has become a "meme," that is, a term or image passed on by experience and imitation. I once drew the diagram in Figure 2.1 on an easel during a kaizen session at a Detroit automaker, and a supervisor spontaneously stood up and shouted, "That's exactly how we operate every week!"

The blame game begins at the top of the diagram, when in good times managers become complacent and consider quality problems and process waste "normal." Their goal is to do just "good enough" to satisfy customers and avoid blame from their boss. And, as long as customers are willing to tolerate delivery delays, sketchy quality, and incrementally higher prices,

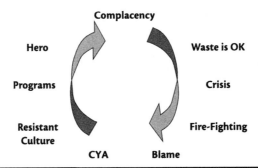

Figure 2.1 The blame game.

wasteful production is tolerated, and it is in reality "OK." It's just business as usual.

When management believes everything is OK, that they're doing good enough, new process waste will eventually trigger a crisis. The crisis might be a missed shipment, a rejected delivery, a lost contract, a financial crunch, a missed project deliverable, a breakdown of a mission-critical system, an environmental catastrophe, or an employee injury or death. When a crisis hits, managers order employees to work around problems, and sooner or later, they find someone else to blame. Back in the day, a factory manager might yell at a worker on the shop floor, or an executive might berate a staff manager in a meeting. However, in the 21st century, public confrontation and harsh language are considered politically incorrect, so pragmatic managers play the blame game in corner offices where they ask, "Who did it?" or "Who should have prevented it?" or "Who hid the problem until it became a crisis?" and of course "Who is to blame?"

Proceeding around the bottom of Figure 2.1, when employees learn that blame is management's game, they practice CYA, cover your "ahem." Searching for a solution, responsible executives may buy a new technology, sponsor training programs, or replace a lower-level manager. But when employees practice CYA, they often resist all improvement programs, even ones intended to help them.

When initial solutions fade or results trend even worse, an executive may designate a "corporate hero" to go onsite and take temporary command of a troubled operation. The incoming hero often has a track record as a turnaround artist within the company or in the industry. The executive empowers the hero to be pragmatic and do whatever it takes to get results back on track and he agrees with his executive sponsor on an empirical target as the definition of success. Early on, a hero might exhibit either a friendly or a tough persona, but in either case, he or she feels free to use both inspirational speeches and fear to push employees hard in order to offset lost time, poor quality, or missing production. He then selects and mobilizes a team of the unit's best managers and specialists, adds outside experts if needed, and the team gathers data, prioritizes problems, identifies causes, does experiments, and applies technical solutions. When they work, the target is hit, and the crisis recedes.

Once the pressure goes off, the finger-pointing begins. For example, one day in a factory that made high-pressure hose for industrial applications, a machine operator warned his supervisor, "I have worked on this machine for a long time, and today it smells bad. I think something is wrong." The weary supervisor called over an engineer to give his expert opinion about the smell. Perhaps he was too busy, or maybe it was just close to lunchtime, because on hearing the employee's concern about the burning smell, he paused, sniffed the air, looked up, and said, "It's just the smell of hamburgers frying at the fast-food restaurant across the street." A few days later, the machine's transmission blew and high-pressure hose production had to be shut down for two weeks while a new one was flown to the United States from a European supplier. Once the new transmission was in place and production was back on line, the supervisor privately blamed the operator for the lost production – the same man who had alerted him about the burning smell from the transmission well before it blew.

After the pragmatic hero achieves the empirical target, he or she may be rewarded with a promotion or move on to attack a new crisis elsewhere. Later, local managers and supervisors naturally consider the hero to be a leadership role model. They have learned that when a problem arises, they are to fight it pragmatically, push employees hard to compensate for operating losses, use metrics to measure progress, and play the blame game whenever deemed necessary.

When executives legitimize the hero model and company managers play the blame game for years or decades, what happens to employee attitudes? One research study surveyed two million employees in over 700 Western companies and found that the quality of an employee's relationship with an immediate manager determined his/her level of engagement and tenure with the enterprise. The researchers concluded that "People join companies and leave managers."[6] When Ackoff's mess of compound problems is mixed with the emotions of management's blame game and employees' CYA, what kind of work environment results? It's an alienated work culture that I'll call "Dilbert's World."

Dilbert's World

Dilbert[7] is the classic cartoon by Scott Adams, and you'll find one posted in many a corporate cubicle or lunchroom. In the strip, the protagonist and his coworkers are a disengaged work group that ridicule their manager, reject his weasel consultants, and find satisfaction in passive cynicism or snarky resistance. Dilbert's boss, Mr. Pointy-Hair, is a selfish, blundering character whose arrogance and blinkered management style are the root cause of the employees' alienation. The cartoon is an amplification of how an egocentric boss creates a disengaged workforce. I call the operating principles of that world, Dilbert's Law:

1. Due to size, scope, and complexity, big enterprises naturally generate lots of waste, problems, and confusion.
2. When managers are unable to resolve problems quickly, they blame employees for them.
3. Management's blame game causes a work culture of disengaged, sometimes alienated employees, extending well beyond those directly criticized.
4. Disengaged, alienated employees ignore problems or willfully cause new ones.
5. Return to number one.

Even though the hero model usually delivers some solutions and short-term improvements, it eventually results in the dysfunctional culture of Dilbert's World. As a result, one survey found that only 21 percent of employees believed that their managers led in a way that motivated them to do outstanding work, and just 15 percent agreed that the leaders in their organization made them enthusiastic about the future.[8] When enterprise executives see these kinds of survey results, you might think they would sponsor a new corporate leadership philosophy and practice. However, most continue to advocate what got them promoted years or decades before.

Reflection: What Can We Learn from Ackoff's Mess?

In the late 20th century, as operations managers faced compound factory problems that were the result of an economic boom in the new systems age, some held fast to command and control and many evolved into the "pragmatic-empirical" management approach. In either case, most continue to rely on blaming people and disengagement continues even today, all be it in more subtle ways. And while business operations are in general cleaner and more organized these days, Ackoff's sets of compound problems still periodically trigger poor quality and process waste in daily work.

In the meantime, Toyota and a few sister companies in Japan applied an Asian leadership philosophy and a practice of continuous improvement in their operations. Their manufacturing sensei taught managers, supervisors, and employees to be mindful of process waste and to apply their innate creativity to find ways to reduce it. Their collective mindfulness and creativity gradually accumulated the kaizen ideas and systems improvements, that evolved into the Toyota Production System (TPS). Hoping to quickly gain similar results, Western managers began benchmarking Toyota's factory layouts, work methods, materials systems, and quality practices. A few of those benchmarking visitors began trying Toyota's factory setup and work methods in some of their operations back home, but without a sensei to show them the way that sustains them.

What You Can Do

You can begin learning about kaizen and the TPS by reading and attending conferences, plus benchmarking companies with successful lean work centers. When the time is right, begin kaizen events or coaching continuous improvement, starting first in receptive work areas. If you're motivated to do so, resolve to become a change leader.

Notes

1 AZ quotes, Russell L. Ackoff.
2 Cited in *Zen in the Ways*, Trevor Leggett, Routledge and Kegan Paul, 1978, p. 197.
3 *Recreating the Corporation*, Russell L. Ackoff, Oxford University Press, 1999, p. 252.
4 *The Revitalization of Alcoa's Tennessee Operations*, Russell L. Ackoff and William B. Deane, National Productivity Review, Summer, 1984, Wiley On-line Library.
5 Modified from *The Moment of Clarity*, Christian Madsbjerg and Mikkel B. Rasmussen, Harvard Business Review Press, 2014, p. 26–27.

6 Cited in *Primal Leadership*, Daniel Goleman, Richard E. Boyatzis, and Annie McKee, Harvard Business Review Press, 1983, p. 83.
7 Author Scott Adams enables use at Dilbert.com, on the 'License Me' button for $19.99.
8 Key Take-Aways from the Gallup Survey of the American Workplace, Lighthouse, A Blog About Leadership & Management Advice, getlighthouse.com.

Chapter 3

Western Business Goes East

Unless we grasp the structure of the Founder's minds, then even though we might be able to copy the Toyota Production System, we wouldn't be able to work out methods to go beyond it, and we couldn't prevail.[1]

Satoshi Hino

When I asked Honda managers how the synchronization of production worked, their answers were always that it wasn't the system, but something about the way they managed their people, something I just couldn't comprehend.[2]

Ken McGuire

IN THE TENNESSEE PLANT

Aiming to fill out its braking offerings to original equipment manufacturers (OEMs) in North America, a multinational automotive parts supplier purchased the Tennessee plant. When one OEM supply chain manager heard the news, he called Chuck the Tennessee plant manager, to deliver a warning to his old friend.

Chuck! The new owners are German and they won't tolerate the mess in your plant.

Chuck went to Charlie, a former union president who was still an informal leader in the plant, to relay the news,

Charlie! he said. We have to show the new owners that we are serious about improving the plant right away.

What do you want to do? Charlie asked.

Well, we ought to start by cleaning up line four, which is the worst – clean all the machines, tools, get the leaks stopped, everything – and then do the rest of the lines as soon as possible, Chuck replied.

Charlie was alert and he wasn't going to be set up to look bad in front of his union brothers, so he challenged: Are you committed to pay the overtime needed to clean line four? Will you stand up and say so in front of everybody?

Chuck responded, I'll do what I gotta' do.

He subsequently agreed to pay 20 union employees do a deep cleaning of line four over the upcoming Christmas shutdown. Line four employees were given the first opportunity to volunteer for the work, and if they declined the hours, other union members could earn the extra pay. At the beginning of the clean-up campaign, one maintenance man told him:

This will never last. You won't stop these machines from leaking in a million years.

You might be right, but our new owners won't tolerate it like it is today, Chuck replied, while shaking his head.

The new owners soon hired a Japanese sensei and his American consultants to teach Tennessee's managers and union employees how to do kaizen and to set up synchronized production work. In order to avoid association with foreign competition, the plant change effort was to be called CIP, the continuous improvement process. Chuck chose Charlie to be the full-time CIP facilitator, and soon after Charlie spoke at an evening union meeting saying: I know that if we continue to have downtime on the lines and pay the air freight costs to fly parts to Detroit overnight, then we're done.

Not long after that a Japanese sensei flew in to Tennessee to lead the first kaizen event. In his wake, his American consultants led kaizen events every month for a couple of years. Charlie followed up on them, led the plant steering committee, and motivated union employees to participate in CIP. Charlie was open and transparent, a tireless advocate for change, a good-old-boy with the street smarts of a big city politician.

As Toyota's reputation for building high-quality, reliable cars grew in the 1980s, Western executives like the Tennessee plant's VP began benchmarking its factory setup and quality methods. Since then, a majority of Western manufacturers have tried to implement them on some scale in one or more of their operations. In order to understand the challenges in starting and, especially, in sustaining new lean operations in a Western business, let's review a bit of recent industrial history.

Benchmarking the Toyota Production System

During the 20th century, Taiichi Ohno and Toyota's outside advisor Shigeo Shingo made kaizen and total quality practices part of every supervisor's and employee's job. Since these practices became part of everyone's standard work, they never gave the resulting system a name, and outsiders just called it "Ohno's Way." Here's the recollection of Professor Robert "Doc" Hall of the time he first learned about it.

> One day a Toyota engineer named Jin-ichirō Nakane called me in my university office. He wanted to bring two or three of his engineers to America to see an inventory management software program called MRP, manufacturing resources planning. So I arranged to take Jin-ichirō and his team to several leading Midwestern companies that were using it in their shop operations. However, as soon as Jin saw how complicated the computerized materials system was, it was obvious to him that Toyota's manual material-pull system was more practical and flexible. During his visit, he talked with me about Toyota's production system and I was fascinated to learn more about how Toyota ran its factories. However, he said that there was nothing much written about it, so he invited me to visit Japan and see it for myself.

When I got to Japan Jin first took me to Kamigo, which was an engine feeder plant for the Toyota assembly plants. This was my aha revelation. The plant was producing 1,400 to 1,500 engines per day, synchronized with assembly plants' schedules. The total lead time from incoming metal to finished car was about 28 hours. The plant was using mostly old equipment from the 1940s and 1950s that had been shipped in from American plants. Kamigo worked two shifts and had 162 employees. The "touch labor" in the plant was only 28 workers. I did some rough calculations and concluded that they were about five times more productive than corresponding American engine manufacturers.[3]

At about that same time, Ken McGuire was part of a benchmarking group that visited multiple Japanese manufacturing companies. After observing the way work was done at Toyota's factories and those of several sister companies, he was so impressed that he later questioned his perception of reality.

During our benchmarking team's first week in Japan, we were scheduled for tours in five or six factories. We were to visit Citizen's Watch, Pentel Pen, Toshiba, and Toyota. On the first day, a reporter from the Japan Times newspaper arrived to give us an orientation to Japanese culture. This was a preview for we first-time visitors on the cultural differences we would witness.

The next day as we toured a factory, we saw defective parts laid out on a conference room table, along with a sign saying: How could this happen? The factory managers and workers were open about such defects because they knew that they wouldn't be blamed for them. They were however, expected to help find the causes and contribute to finding a solution for quality problems. Each one was here that I first heard the managers say that "a defect is a treasure." A defect was considered by them as a way to identify a root cause and resolve it with a process improvement. This was my aha moment. The factory efficiencies we could see were not inherently cultural, but they were due to how the factories were led and managed every day.

In American plants, production machines and processes were designed to be complex and were highly efficient "on paper." But when we actually tried to run such complex processes at a fast pace, production was slowed by various disruptions. At the Toyota factory, they did things on a slower, more deliberate rhythm, one planned and synchronized to the rate of customer deliveries. Their supervisors and cross-functional support staff responded to issues quickly and mitigated every line slowdown, machine breakdown, or quality problem soon after it was flagged by front-line employees. Running with a predictable pace and quick responses to arising problems, the lines didn't need much inventory and they consistently hit their production goals. These are both big wins for any manufacturing operation.

At one meeting a plant manager explained to us that profit was what was left after subtracting materials plus labor and overhead from the price set by the market. This was a truly foreign concept to us, since we were accustomed to raising our rates above costs in order to create profit. Gradually, we realized that it wasn't just what the Japanese companies were doing that made them so competitive; it was the way that we American managers were thinking that was causing our costs to be so high!

Another group member and I arranged for everyone to share our individual notes on each factory. There was some skepticism about the claims of the Japanese managers we heard, yet we couldn't deny that what we saw was working well. We were all operating folks who would not be easily fooled by gimmicks, and what we saw there were shop-floor production practices that just made sense. We couldn't understand the underlying source of their manufacturing advantage, but we knew it was true.

Later on that same trip we visited Honda. There we saw an even faster pace for production, and their quality was just as good as Toyota's. Each time we went into meetings with a Japanese plant manager to discuss technical process capability, their answers were always that it wasn't the sys-tem, but something about the way they managed their people, something I just couldn't comprehend, they said: Machines should work, and people should think. On our return from the study mission we summarized four concepts from our trip at an American conference:

- Inventory is evil
- A defect is a treasure
- People are all engaged and on the same page
- Continuous pursuit of excellence is real

Our team told the conference attendees that the Japanese manufacturing companies were really very good, but the audience didn't believe us. They just wanted to think that the Japanese companies were cheating somehow, or were rigging their currency to beat American companies on price.

After being challenged at the conference, our tour group members began to wonder if maybe the Japanese managers had tricked us. So the next spring, we went to some of the same companies a second time, and visited their supplier's factories as well. On that tour, we saw production and quality performance that was even scarier. We learned that the best companies in Japan only did business with the best suppliers. If a supplier wasn't yet approved to supply with a top company it had to exaggerate its Toyota production and quality practices to even be considered as a long-term supplier. They were working doubly hard, just hoping to become a permanent part of an OEM's supply chain. After a few days touring factories on that second trip, I spoke up and said: Hey, this is real![4]

A few American and European executives, plant managers, and operations leaders, the "early-adopters," returned from Japan and applied Toyota's factory setup and work methods in their own operations, and early word-of-mouth success stories spread. Some paid Japanese sensei to fly across big oceans to teach their American and European managers how to setup Toyota-style production lines, work cells, and quality practices. Since the Japanese sensei were typically onsite for only a week, they sped up their teaching approach into what was called a "kaizen blitz." Art Byrne is a former CEO and author, and he recalls his first experience with Japanese Sensei Iwata at one of his company's plants this way:[5]

We had planned to begin a kaizen event in a conference room with an American-style presentation on how our machines produced the parts, followed by a plant tour. When we started the presentation Sensei Iwata quickly stopped us and said: We know how the machines work, let's cut this presentation. So we suggested, How about doing the plant tour? We went out onto the shop floor and got about 100 yards when stopped us and he said: I've seen enough. When we returned to the conference room Sensei Iwata wrote on the board in huge letters "NO GOOD." Then, he challenged us through the translator: Everything here is no good, what do you want to do about it?

After a brief discussion, we agreed to consider changes and he formed us into two teams. We told him that the most important machines were the big industrial chucks, so he sent his partner and the first team of six or eight over to work on him. Then, Sensei Iwata said: I like assembly, so the rest of us went with him. In assembly we found four people making components on a conveyor belt, and he immediately ordered us to get rid of the belt. We looked at each other in disbelief. So as the responsible executive and based solely on my faith in his reputation, I said "OK." And then, BANG, we were off and running. Our team began to use tools and break down the conveyor line with the sensei pushing us all the way.

A bit later, one of the company managers who had gone over to the machining side came running over saying that the other sensei had his sleeves rolled up and was driving a forklift. He wanted the Americans to use pry bars and help him move eight large machines over the lunch hour, placing them close together and in a sequential order on the floor.

At the end of that first day, sensei Iwata showed us how to time and run the restructured lines as synchronized work cells. All of this was far beyond our traditional belief that plant change had to be slow and methodical. We were shocked that it was possible to make so much change so fast.[6]

Not long after the events in Art's story took place, one of the most important experiments in industrial history began at a shuttered GM assembly plant in California. There, Toyota partnered with General Motors in a joint venture called the New United Motor Manufacturing or NUMMI. It was Toyota's first attempt to manage an automotive assembly operation in the United States. Its leaders were uncertain whether they could make the Toyota Production System succeed outside Japan, and they studied every inch of the plant every day.[7] They realized that in order to be a global player, they needed to learn how to make Americans work as effectively as their Japanese counterparts. John Shook was an American employee at Toyota headquarters in Japan at that time, and he traveled to the NUMMI plant to support training. He describes that period of time this way:[8]

Toyota hired me in late 1983 to work on the Toyota side of its new venture with GM early on when it still lacked a name. I was assigned to a newly formed group at the company's Toyota City headquarters that was tasked to develop and deliver training programs to support its looming overseas expansion.

The GM California plant had been considered the worst in its manufacturing system. When the factory reopened under Toyota's guidance, each assembly line worker was given the knowledge and skills required to complete his or her standard work tasks. When a problem occurred, some abnormality that prevented a job performer from doing the work successfully, he or she could pull a rope located overhead, and a number would light up on a board, signaling the team leader that a worker was experiencing a problem. The factory workforce had received a promise from management that whenever they had a problem completing their standard work, the team leader would immediately come to their aid. That's quite a big promise to a workforce of a couple thousand, and the job cycles were in the neighborhood of one minute on each task. But, Toyota knew that management's commitment to helping was what it took to enable workers to build in quality and engage people in problem-solving and making improvements.

While it wasn't easy, it was remarkably successful. Toyota, NUMMI, the UAW, and the entire workforce working together achieved Toyota City levels of performance through an extraordinary degree of mutual trust. In terms of actual performance, NUMMI didn't just improve; it went from GM's worst plant to its very best. That improvement was achieved in just one year, and with the same workforce.

Wanting to Drive Like Toyota, Western Business Has Spent 30 Years Looking for the Keys

When the book *Lean Thinking* was published, enthusiasm for Toyota's lean system ignited an explosion of kaizen events across Western industry. Yet over the past two decades, Western executives and managers have struggled to sustain the promising early results of kaizen events in their facilities. David Verble, a former continuous improvement coach at Toyota in Kentucky, described the challenge that Western executives face in getting their managers and supervisors to sustain lean production this way:

> The challenges managers face in making the transition from being traditional managers to becoming continuous improvement leaders are many and huge. It is essential to bring those challenges into the open and lead our organizations in finding ways to address them if we are to achieve the lean/continuous improvement culture we aspire to. Our habits as knowers and fixers are deeply ingrained in us and in our culture as a whole.[9]

Reflection: What Can We Learn from Western Business Going East?

Why couldn't those early Western benchmarking visitors comprehend what made Toyota's lean system so successful? Author Roger J. Davies describes the source of our Western confusion this way: "Japanese culture is conceived as a structure composed of successive layers, in which new strata are super-imposed on the old."[10] As Japanese industrial companies rebuilt in the mid-20th century after the war, their executives layered the American business model on top of their centuries-old cultural and spiritual beliefs. In this way, a series of Toyoda family CEOs fused the Western business model with their Buddhist philosophy and evolved the company's leadership approach and a practice of continuous improvement.[11]

Western visitors to Japan's top manufacturers couldn't see the lower layers of the sensei's teaching approach, one that used improving the work itself as the vehicle to develop everyone into a change leader. The sensei knew how to evoke the first key to a lean operations transformation, kaizen mind.

What You Can Do

Read the next four chapters on the other keys to a lean business transformation.

Notes

1 Inside the Mind of Toyota, S. Hino, op. cit., p. xi.
2 Ken McGuire, Management Excellence Action Coalition interview in 2011.
3 Robert "Doc" Hall interview in 2011.
4 Ken McGuire, Management Excellence Action Coalition interview in 2011.
5 At Jacobs Manufacturing Corporation, Part of the Danaher Company, The Lean Post, LEI.org, June 11, 2018.
6 Art Byrne interview and The Lean Post, LEI.org, May 7, 2018.
7 Jeff Liker email, 2/14/2019.
8 This was hyperlinked to: https://www.lean.org/lexicon/work.
9 *Leader's Actions Speak but Their Talk Matters Too*, David Verble, Lean Enterprise Institute, 2009, p. 2.
10 *Japanese Culture*, Roger J. Davies, Tuttle Publishing, 2016, p. 31.
11 At age 11, Sakichi Toyoda's family sent him to attend the local Buddhist temple of Seicho-ji where he learned about Nichiren, Pure Land Buddhism, and Zen. Author Steven Batchelor writes that Nichiren Buddhism's central belief was that, "the Buddha is immanent within each moment of life is the basic core of Zen."

Chapter 4

The First Key Is Kaizen Mind

At some point, a light comes on, and you feel that keeping it simple, using your mind, and insisting on experiments all the time is at the heart of all this.[1]

Andrew Dillon

I just figured it out, what you have been telling us. I've been waiting for you to give us an answer, and actually, no one knows it![2]

A Kaizen Participant

IN THE TENNESSEE PLANT

The North American vice president challenged the Tennessee plant manager, Ron, to upgrade the facility and implement Toyota-style production across the plant. He told him that he would invest in new equipment and pay the consultant costs and overtime pay needed to involve employees in a continuous improvement program (CIP). A week or so later, Ron and his leadership team joined the plant's union leaders for a day-long discussion on a future vision for the plant. Afterwards, Ron said: At the end of the day, the union leaders and I agreed on many things. Plant survival was the common ground, and I can always go back to that future vision to barter or negotiate and make progress. Ron and the union president signed an agreement for equal participation in the continuous improvement program, formed a joint steering committee and named Charlie, a former union president, as the program's facilitator. American lean consultants flew in and led monthly kaizen events. Charlie followed up on improvement projects and resolved any job classification or safety issues that arose. For example, in one CIP event, both employees and engineers agreed that the critical Petra machine could never hold Toyota's tight part tolerance for brakes, and he allocated the money to replace it right away. In another, a team decided that an old paint system, one that had been fixed many times before, would never work well enough to deliver quality to modern customers. The next day Ron procured the funds and ordered a new one. He empowered all employees to participate in CIP and suggest ways to reduce waste in their jobs and the set up in their work area. His commitment to the plant's survival and strong leadership in procuring financial resources led many union employees to buy-in. A plant transformation was underway.

The Tennessee auto-parts plant was built during the postwar economic boom in America, and it was set up along the lines of Taylorism, that is structured with narrow, timed jobs and quality assured by inspectors and managed with the traditional command and control approach. As I worked monthly at the plant over a few years, I gradually learned the five keys to a lean business transformation. The table below, and similar ones in the next four chapters, each define a sequence of logic around a key to a lean business transformation using the format of: "the problem to solve," the chapter's "key" to solving it, "what leaders do" when they turn each key, and last, how each key corresponds to one of the "challenges" in the classic book *The Leadership Challenge* by James M. Kouzes and Barry Z. Posner.[3] The first key is kaizen mind.

Problem to Solve	Key	What Leaders Do	Leadership Challenge
Ackoff's mess	Kaizen mind	Use kaizen events to evoke kaizen mind	Challenge the process

Kaizen Mind

These days "kaizen" is a well-known Japanese term, one that typically translates to "good change" or "change for the better." Author Masaaki Imai first introduced kaizen to a Western audience in his book *Kaizen: The Key to Japan's Competitive Success*,[4] and he defined it as: "small changes, involving everyone, that don't cost a lot of money."

During the 1950s, Mr. Imai had worked for the Japan Productivity Center in Washington, D.C. His job there was to take Japanese visitors on benchmarking tours that were advertised as opportunities to see: "the secret of American industrial productivity." One year a repeat visitor to an American plant said to Imai: "You know, this factory makes its products exactly the same way it did on my previous visit some years ago." Reflecting on the visitor's comment, Imai concluded: "I have reached the conclusion that the kaizen concept is nonexistent or at least very weak in most Western companies today. Worse yet, they reject it without knowing what it really entails."

After publishing his first book, Mr. Imai began receiving requests for consulting help from North American companies, and he signed on a cadre of kaizen consultants (of which I was one). The consultants later broke down his kaizen idea into the following six concepts:[5] (1) What the work is counts. Understand it in detail; (2) Identify the waste; (3) What customers want counts; Understand their requirements in detail; (4) Define a future state – what does success look like? (5) Empower and engage the team to operationalize ways to take waste out of their jobs; (6) You have to have faith in the process that by asking questions in the right order, you'll succeed.

The consultants' goal was to teach participants how to use kaizen to redesign their own jobs and factory set up in order to eliminate waste and produce high-quality products and/or services smoothly and on time for customers. The consultants would typically plan a kaizen event by selecting a work process with a lot of waste, ask the responsible manager to form a kaizen team plus dedicate technical support specialists for a few days or a week. They used a Zen approach in leading kaizen events, that is, they gave the team a brief orientation to process waste, then quickly threw them into a challenge that was over their heads, offered little or no help, and expected them to become mindful of the on-going work. There are three kinds of kaizen. The first is a 5S kaizen, in which a coach or facilitator guides local employees to create a clean, organized area, where effective process work can be done.

5S Kaizen: Workplace Order and Organization

A 5S workshop is a deep cleaning and organization of a work area or whole facility. It must be sponsored by a plant or operations manager, led by a facilitator, and done by the work area's employees. It focuses on five sequential concepts which translate from Japanese as: "separate and sort," "scrub and shine," "straighten," "standardize," and "sustain."[6] Here's an example of a simple 5S kaizen in a real estate office.

> I was hired to do a one-day process kaizen on the sales process in a real estate office, but once there I found the office to be such a mess that I shifted the event to a 5S. After a brief orientation to the 5Ss, I asked the salespeople to begin cleaning their desks, organizing their files, and then proceed to clean and organize a chaotic storage room. One sales associate looked at me forlornly and asked, "Are you really going to make us do this?" Indeed I was, and they did. The sales process kaizen waited for another day.

The steps for planning a 5S kaizen in a big operation include: (1) reference a company, plant, or operation's vision for broad goals and guidelines; (2) draft specific goals unique for a facility; (3) set up a steering committee to plan consistent 5S events, audit, and follow up; (4) designate a 5S coordinator and define their duties and term; (5) develop a strategy for each area in a facility, taking into account existing time and resources; (6) prepare by purchasing cabinets, shelving, label makers, cleaning tools, hanging boards, and other supplies unique to the business; (7) orient managers and employees in the target process and areas adjoining it; (8) conduct a safety orientation; (9) start the first three Ss in the target work area, storage area, or public space; (10) concurrently with the first three Ss, draft checklists for periodic cleaning to be used in the future; and (11) make audit sheets for subsequent 5S audits to provide feedback to ensure the fourth and fifth Ss. In addition to the benefits of cleaning and organizing, a 5S kaizen can be a team-building exercise. Here's an example of a 5S kaizen in a furniture production factory with only 20 employees.

> In the furniture factory, employees made craftsman-style tables and book cases. The sequence of work stations was: receive rough-sawn lumber; then plane and cut the boards to standard sizes; move finished boards to the next station where joints are glued

and cleaned; on to sand and varnish; and finally, move to pack and ship at the loading dock.

At the time the plant was so busy that shutting down production for a full day of 5S wasn't a good option. So the plant manager and I strategized a way to schedule 5S activity. All employees were to work on 5S on Tuesday and Thursday for several weeks. Each clean-up period focused all 20 employees on a single work station for 30 minutes twice each week, and then moved on to another work station the following week. Rather than cleaning at the end of the shift when employees are anxious to go home, the half-hour cleaning was scheduled just before lunch. As the employees helped clean and organize one another's work areas, the 5S project became a team-building exercise.

Figure 4.1 shows before and after pictures of the impact of a 5S at a work station in the furniture factory.

Figure 4.1   Before and after 5S kaizen.

An initial 5S exercise is an easy thing to do, but the problem is, only few production managers are willing to dedicate actual production time to sustain it. Below is an example of an initial 5S workshop from a maintenance manager at a Canadian company where employees bought in, but the operations manager later didn't support continuing it.[7]

Our 5S workshop was a great learning experience. The employees on the team followed a hands-on approach and learned what 5S entails. Initially, I was under the assumption that it would be strictly cleaning up, but as I walked around talking with the coach, I saw that the ultimate goal of 5S is to improve the flow of work.

We can save a lot of money by achieving a steady flow in production. Sustaining a clean and orderly workplace is the hardest part, of course. As part of everyone's standard work, we set up a 15-minute shift overlap of the day and night shifts. They had been blaming each other for not completing their 5S work at shift change, and the overlap eliminated some of the built-up animosity between shifts. The 5S also improved safety because people no longer had to walk on dirty floors or step over misplaced materials. The checklists are being done at shift turnover; however, cleaning during the shifts is not happening.

I made the case to my upper management that we would benefit from allowing employees to do 5S workshops in all facilities. However, our production managers were so focused on the schedule that they wouldn't give up any production time to do them. As a result, at this time, we haven't introduced 5S at our other facilities, and that is disappointing. Still, what we accomplished in our first 5S standardization has held up fairly well and was a huge stepping stone for our company moving forward.

When employees complete a successful 5S kaizen, they begin to discover their kaizen minds, and as a result, many are then motivated to do a process kaizen event. There are two versions of process kaizen.

Two Types of Process Kaizen: Maintenance and Improvement

The second and third kinds of kaizen aim to improve the process itself. The second is a "maintenance" kaizen, that is an improvement that focuses on recovering lost process performance. Third, an "improvement" kaizen focuses on raising existing performance beyond the current process standard. In both, a facilitator initially orients a kaizen team to the process wastes of: (1) overprocessing – doing either unnecessary work or a process that does more than required; (2) transportation – conveying people or things without value or moving unnecessary items; (3) motion – unnecessary movement of people or materials and moving too quickly or slowly; (4) inventory – storing excessive supplies, materials, equipment, or information; (5) overproduction – producing something at the wrong time or in unnecessary amounts; (6) time – waiting for people and information or idle time; (7) defects and rework – problems with material or product quality; and (8) people – underutilizing employees' skills and creativity. In the case below, Dr. John Drogosz describes a time when he initiated a single kaizen improvement that eliminated waiting for its customer to supply work.[8]

> When I started working for a pattern shop, it seemed like every day was a balancing act. On some weekday mornings, the customers sent us a large number of patterns needing adjustment and repair. At other times, they dumped them into our shop on Fridays because they wanted to make sure we had them and were accountable to return them in time for their production run the next week. When this happened, our company paid overtime rates to complete them on that weekend. It didn't make any sense. I got to know the customer's engineers who led the repairs and I asked them,
>
> Is there a schedule? And is it solid?
>
> Yes, they said, looking curious as to why I would ask.
>
> Is it secret? I probed.
>
> No, came their answer.
>
> Can we get it to anticipate our workload, so we know what's coming and can get going easier? I asked, carefully.
>
> Sure, the customer engineer said readily.
>
> That was easy, I said to myself.
>
> So, with the next week's schedule in hand, my company was able to set up, balance, and sequence the work to produce exactly what they needed in their production sequence throughout the week. We drove our own truck the short distance to pick up the set of patterns ourselves, repaired them, and took them back daily. The lesson was that either you can act like a victim or understand the waste in your situation and change it.

A Process Kaizen Event

During a process kaizen event, the aim can be either to recover the lost performance or to redesign the work so that it can achieve a higher standard. A kaizen team initially observes an area's work, lists its waste and problems, and then sorts the issues into two piles. The first is composed of issues that the local team can work on immediately on their own, perhaps with a little help from maintenance, engineering, quality, IT, and others. The second stack is made up of quality problems or waste that originates in other departments or that require investment in new machinery or need a change in a management policy, and they are set aside pending executive approval to work on them. The team brainstorms ideas to counter or eliminate priorities in the first stack and try them, immediately if possible. The picture in Figure 4.2 was taken by a kaizen team as they used cardboard to locate machines to test the transportation and ergonomics of a new machining line.

Figure 4.2   Process kaizen event.

One corporation that has invested in kaizen for decades is Standard Products. The company embraced the kaizen approach early on and recently cited having held kaizen events in 39 plants worldwide.[9] They report that a typical kaizen workshop resulted in a 25–30 percent improvement in production and 80–85 percent reductions in work-in-process inventory. Here are sections of a report by a company engineer who participated in an early kaizen event.[10]

> Previously, factory engineers had made numerous efficiency improve-
> ments on the Ford line, and they considered it done. However, in
> a four-day blitz, the kaizen team followed the process of PDCA,
> the plan-do-check-adjust model, and they found a great deal more
> improvement than we imagined possible. In the event, management
> set improvement goals, and the team identified waste, prioritized

issues, brainstormed improvement ideas, made a plan, executed
it, checked results, made adjustments to the line design, and then
repeated the cycle on a next improvement. The kaizen team, fully
supported by engineers and maintenance staff, was able to produce 18
percent more quality parts per day with an 18.2 percent reduction in
headcount, and yet by prior agreement, no one was laid off. The team
realized savings in raw and work-in-process inventory and numerous
other improvements in quality and safety. Neither we engineers nor
the plant's managers anticipated that such a radical change in the line
would be so readily accepted by employees. Afterward, the team summarized the following guidelines for success in a kaizen event report:

■ Use the simple, easy-to-understand concepts presented about eliminat-
  ing waste.
■ Be patient but persistent; work with the team not against it.
■ Keep the team involved, set goals, and adjust the design as you go.
■ Follow up on all changes, completing Plan, Do, Check, Act on each.
■ Support groups are specialists in their field; operators are specialists at
  their job.
■ Success results when the two join in cooperation and understanding.
■ Incorporating work-cell concepts with ownership by work teams is an
  absolute must.
■ The participative approach is challenging for all involved, but doing
  kaizen is rewarding and will keep companies sharp, competitive, and
  successful.

In the 21st century, kaizen is still a new idea to many entrepreneurs, small
business founders, job-shop managers, restaurant owners, and others. Cyd's on
the Park is a restaurant that has been recognized by *USA Today* for its contemporary concept and great food. Cyd is the restaurant's founder, and she,
along with her manager, applied kaizen to the arrangement of the tables to
allow better traffic flow and table access for servers. She later led kaizen with
the cooks who improved their work stations and reorganized the food storage
area for easier access. Afterward, she described the value of kaizen this way:[11]

> In my experience, the value of the kaizen method is threefold. First,
> instead of having management make all the decisions, it allowed
> me to include my staff in a planning process. Second, it created a
> team-building experience for my staff. Third, it enabled the team to

discover improvements for the operation that benefit the customers. We began in the front service area, reorganizing tables, relocating the water and condiments cabinet, and creating a new aisle. When kaizen caught on with the cooks they found ways to bring order to the work in the kitchen and organized ready access to food in the storage areas, reducing time and cutting overall food cost. Doing kaizen resulted not only in making our restaurant more efficient but participation led the staff to embrace the changes. Working "inside-out", that is, focusing on their mental engagement first and then identifying physical changes, enabled true continuous improvement.

While doing kaizen motivates most employees, a few will resist participation for personal reasons. Here's an example of a time a production employee resisted participation in process kaizen, until a coworker changed his mind.

The shop employees trudged up into a conference room for a two-day kaizen event. As I began speaking up front, one young man, whom I'll call Mr. Smith, wasn't having it. He tipped his baseball cap down over his eyes, slid his seat back, and placed his dirty boots on top of the narrow conference room table in front of him. I didn't know what to do, but I couldn't ignore his protest. But rather than use my authority as the event leader to force him to change or leave the event, I suspended judgment and just became mindful. I moved directly in front of Mr. Smith's position at the narrow table and waited. He kept his hat over his eyes, avoiding mine. I took a couple of deep breaths, let go of my fight-or-flight instinct, and accepted his protest as the reality of the moment. I was not uncomfortable with the uncertainty because I knew that if I stayed present, sooner or later a rising intuition would tell me what to do. When one did arrive it told me to tap his dirty boot and ask:

What's the deal with you?

This kaizen stuff is all a bunch of bullshit, he mumbled from beneath his hat visor.

Maybe, maybe not, I volleyed back, purposely offering an ambiguous response to leave the pressure on him. He didn't respond.

Since his protest was right at the beginning of the kaizen event, his ax to grind came from the past. Perhaps he had unfinished business with a manager or had previously experienced a bungled factory change. The other team members waited and fidgeted in their chairs. I didn't intend to let him out of the trouble he gotten himself into, nor was I going to allow him to leave and become some sort of factory-resistance hero. I said nothing, just stayed mindful by tracking my in-and-out breath. I knew that by being present, I'd soon see something new arise in the reality of the situation.

It always does.

Finally, stepping into the leadership space I'd intentionally left empty, a female team member seated two seats away from Mr. Smith took the lead. She delivered powerful feedback, saying: You know, you do this all the time in the plant and now you're doing it here. You just complain and you don't do anything to help anyone. We're all sick of it, so straighten up!

There was a pregnant pause in the room. The woman's eyes didn't move from Mr. Smith's hat visor and were so intense I thought that they might burn a hole in it. She had called him out with the credibility of a co-worker, and she wasn't about to back down. I had nothing useful to add. After a few more seconds of tense silence, her will broke his will. Mr. Smith slowly sat the front legs of his chair down, put his dirty boots back on the floor, raised his hat visor a bit, sat up kind of straight, and stared directly ahead. Taking this as a sign of victory, yet without saying an unkind word, I walked back to the front of the room to resume the event.

Mr. Smith didn't participate much that day or the next, but that wasn't the end of the story. The following month on my trip in to follow up on the new work cell startup, I wondered what new challenge Mr. Smith might offer this time. Imagine my shock when I arrived and heard that not only had Mr. Smith accepted the new work cell but that he had been elected its first team leader! I was stunned. I had a meeting with the team later that morning and Mr. Smith spoke positively about the new work set up. I didn't bring up his disruptive behavior the month before. Over the ensuing month he had discovered kaizen mind.

Once a critical mass of employees in an operation have done kaizen, most will have developed kaizen mind, and they will continue to challenge the status quo in operations, even without prompting from managers. What could possibly be wrong with that?

As it turns out, quite a lot.

Reflection: What Can We Learn from Kaizen Mind

The purpose of kaizen is to eliminate process waste in the work itself, and to develop kaizen mind in all employees. However, similar to the idea of brainstorming, a kaizen event is a freewheeling improvement session that by its nature can result in a random pattern of improvements, a "shotgun" approach, a list of good ideas that won't readily align to accumulate more value for end customers. What does? The second key to transforming a Western business into a lean operation is lean thinking.

What You Can Do

Plan and conduct a service or knowledge work improvement session using my Kaizen Event Facilitator's Guide.[12] Orient your managers to understand that the goal of kaizen isn't just improved work methods, but developing kaizen mind in all employees.

Notes

1 Interview with Andrew Dillon 2014.
2 Kaizen event comment reported by Tom Lane.
3 *The Leadership Challenge* 4th Edition, James M. Kouzes and Barry Z. Posner John Wiley & Sons, 2007, p. 26.
4 *Kaizen, The Key to Japan's Competitive Success*, Masaaki Imai, McGraw-Hill, 1986.
5 Kaizen Institute presentation material used in North America.
6 Seri – separate and sort; Seiton – Set in order; Seiso – Shine; Seiketsu – Standardize; Shitsuke – Sustain.
7 The maintenance manager later reported that the company invested in kaizen and made significant progress.
8 Case from John Drogosz, Vice President of Optiprise Consulting.
9 Standard Products Co. has done events at all 39 of its plants worldwide. Industry Week, by Mark H. Sheridan, December 21, 2004.
10 Taken from a report written by an anonymous engineer at one Standard Products plant.
11 Cyd Henrikson is the founder of Cyd's in the Park, a contemporary café in Peoria, IL.
12 https://blog.lucidmeetings.com/hubfs/facilitator-guides/Value-Stream-Mapping-Facilitators-Guide.pdf.

Chapter 5

The Second Key Is Lean Thinking

Technological thinking is a marvelous thing, but it is its very success that must be feared because it so captivates, bewitches, dazzles and beguiles that it threatens to someday become accepted and practiced as the only way of thinking.[1]

Albert Low

We've spent years and millions of dollars on our company-branded lean production system, and we still have to make employees do it.[2]

American Executive

IN THE TENNESSEE PLANT

Ron had arrived in Tennessee with a reputation as a tough, plant turnaround guy. He could be jovial and engaging in person, but his aggressive nature was never far below the surface. He had been a football linebacker in high school, and his body language told even the toughest guys in the plant that he wouldn't run away from a fight. Like many engineers, he placed a priority on maintaining the facility and equipment, and he became angry when he saw employees neglect their machines. In our monthly one-on-one coaching meetings, I told him that his angry outbursts at people on the shop floor were a barrier to continuous improvement, yet talk alone couldn't change his emotional reactions to dirty equipment. What finally changed his mind was participating in a day long visioning session in which he and the union leaders discussed the future of the plant. While walking and talking on the shop floor that day, they found a common purpose, that of saving the plant and sustaining its 400 good manufacturing jobs. One afternoon soon after, I walked the shop floor to touch base with a couple of my favorite employees. Wormy was running a semi-automated machine, and after we chatted a bit, he asked: What's going to happen to my job? I said: The company is committed in CIP to improve the jobs, and no one will be laid off due to process improvements. Continuing my walk, I next checked in with Paul, who was a tough, smart, and skeptical union leader. He challenged me asking, What are you doing here? I bet that it's just to make a lot of money! I'd heard this from him before and holding steady eye contact I said: Paul, I need you to back the f*** off. After a brief pause, he smiled and said: I was wondering if we in the union could trust you to be honest. You passed the test today.

Over the past three decades, tens of thousands of plant managers like Ron have sponsored kaizen events, and most have shown great potential results, yet they rarely align improvements all the way through a product value stream. Lean thinking enables executives and leadership teams to develop an operational vision, which in turn enables managers to value steam map the work, prioritize kaizen ideas and set up lean systems. The second key to transforming a Western business into a lean operation is lean thinking.

Problem to Solve	Key	What Leaders Do	Leadership Challenge
Kaizen doesn't align a flow of customer value	Lean thinking	Envision lean operations	Inspire a shared vision

Lean Thinking

The publication of the book *Learning to See* gave executives, plant managers, and change leaders a way to envision a future-state product value stream or an operating facility and plan improvements that would deliver more value to customers.

A typical value stream mapping format is shown in Figure 5.1. It pictures a factory product flow, boxes for data to be collected at each work station, and a horizontal ladder that accumulates the total throughput time. Once a current state is mapped, analyzed, and its root problems are addressed by proposed changes, a business or site leadership team can envision a future state.

Mapping begins by grouping similar products or services in order to itemize the value streams in an operation. A value stream can be based on selected characteristics, materials, process routings, seasonal demand, or other unique business factors. For example, consider the brakes manufactured for cars. Passenger car brake pads are semimetallic and look similar to the ceramic pads made for high-performance vehicles, but they don't share material, equipment,

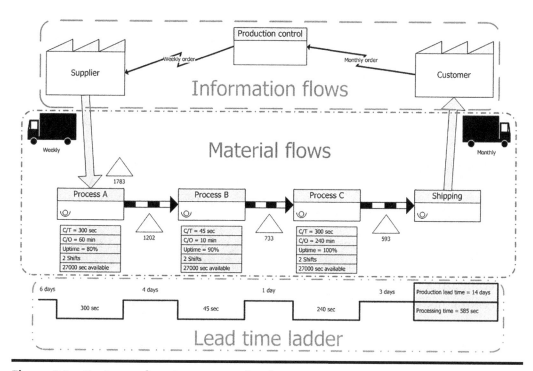

Figure 5.1   Factory value stream mapping format.

or a process routing. Therefore, the two look-alike products are not members of the same family but members of two different value streams. Authors John Drew, Blair McCallum, and Stefan Roggenhofer describe a number of concepts useful for designing a lean product value stream.[3]

- Create value streams by grouping similar products or services.
- Design work tasks and processes that allow the value to flow along the stream from beginning to end.
- Pull products where the flow must be broken.
- Flex the operation to match customer demand.
- Introduce information defining customer requirements at a single point and as late as possible in the process.
- Standardize operations to create a foundation for flexibility.
- Detect and fix abnormalities as close as possible to the point where they occur.

Once a business or value stream team has drafted a future-state vision, they can charter improvement events or specify coaching targets aimed to reduce or eliminate big wastes or systems constraints in strategic work locations. In the case below, lean coach Mike Funke partnered with an area production manager and his team leads to plan a lean event timed to relieve the company's biggest constraint operation.

> I was supporting the molding department manager and his young team leaders in an effort to improve production in a 100-year-old steel foundry. On a Saturday, we met and discussed how to focus an initial lean improvement event. In our discussion, the young management team leads joked about the molding crew's "cowboy" mentality, yet I admired their knowledge and experience. However, when I asked the team leads to help me roll out the company's Toyota-lean production effort in molding, they all said that it was bullshit, just another management flavor of the month. Given the company's past starts and stops in its internal lean program, their comments were justified. However, the molding manager was always catching hell for running late on the schedule and everyone finally agreed because they knew that the department had to improve its performance.
>
> During that initial discussion, we set three goals: to make the workflow steady; to make the work easier to do; and to make

daily production visual so that the team could self-manage and hit the daily schedule. We also agreed to involve the crew in improving their own work so that they would sustain the changes. We joked that the our first rule was: We're not going do anything stupid. We intended to apply lean principles sensibly, that is, we would not implement anything just for the sake of trying a lean tool. When I next met with the leads, my first question was: How do you know if the area has had a good day or a bad day? After talking this over, they came up with three characteristics of a good day:

- Everyone going home safely at the end of the workday
- Hitting our production target/pitch for melting and pouring
- Having no major metallurgical or physical issues in the products produced

As I said, the molding cowboys were all long-term, strong-minded, older guys who had earned high status in the company because they poured molten steel alloys into large intricate molds, one of the toughest jobs in the shop. Later, I asked the crew to meet me between shifts to discuss both the good days and bad days, and with some prompting, they agreed to do so. When the crew reported having had a bad day in these discussions, I would ask them to identify the most significant barriers that arose during the shift, what the cause of each might be, and how we might make sure that each one would never happen again. It was a rudimentary PDCA, and at times it made my gut ache, but in it, everyone's energy focused on learning how to make things better. These initial conversations built a foundation of trust for success on their upcoming lean journey.

We spent the first day of the actual lean event observing the crew at work and seeing the problems that, in their opinion, were barriers to having a good day. At the time, the molding shop was an open floor area with three dedicated crews simultaneously making huge, semi-customized steel parts. The crew could build three sets of molds a week on a consistent basis, sometimes four, but we needed between five and six sets in order to match demand. As a result, customer lead time had grown out beyond 40 weeks. When we observed the work and talked with the crew, it became clear that the area struggled because of lost time on the critical molder job.

On the second day, after some frustrating discussions, I finally asked the cowboys if they needed six sets of parts a week, why didn't they just make one set a day for six days? Of course, they had a lot of "explanations" about how that had never been done before, and why it couldn't be done, and so on. I batted away all their excuses, and they finally agreed that the ideal would be to build one complete mold per day. In the follow-on discussion, they detailed a vision of the operation. They would make the bottom half of a mold, called the drag, on the first shift; make the top half, the cope, on the second shift; and then make the last part, the shake, on the third shift. The vision leveled the schedule and enabled a kan-ban pull signal to bring component materials to each shift team just-in-time. We set up a visual method for them to track production in two-hour intervals so that if they fell behind, they could troubleshoot the constraint and make adjustments during the shift.

Based on this operational vision, each shift defined the preparation needed to fabricate their part. By combining everyone's "best known ways" together, they determined their standard work practices, and everyone agreed to use the standard work to make their component for a set. The young team leaders then worked back from the new standard work and drafted a training plan that would enable the crew members to complete the work needed on one shift. At the end of the multi-week effort, everyone coalesced around the new vision. At that point, even the most resistant cowboy saw that the leveled workflow, planning, new standard work, and the training just made sense. It was the tightest, most integrated system of lean production I had ever seen, with a level schedule, work standards drafted by the actual workers, and a related training plan.

Later, the crew proudly presented the new molding process design to company top executives who approved the plan and congratulated them on their efforts. When it kicked off, the new lean operation worked right away, and it ran as planned over the following three years. It consistently achieved the target of a "mold a day," achieving a nearly 50 percent increase in output with the same staffing, plus it delivered gains in safety, quality, and cost. The lean event transformed the molding process, a constraint department that had previously been considered impossible to standardize and improve. The key was keeping it practical, focusing on the improving the work itself, collaborating with the cowboys, and trusting them to apply their natural creative energies.

Sustaining commitment to lean work among pioneers like the cowboys requires supervisors and technical support specialists to deliver the quick expertise and resources needed to resolve arising problems – issues that can discredit the change. However, department managers in functions such as maintenance, information technology, manufacturing engineering, and quality control (and others unique to a business) are typically rewarded for annual goals and long-term projects within their functional "silo." Below is a case of a time when one plant maintenance manager didn't want to support someone's lean event; mine.

> On Wednesday morning of a week-long lean event, the team for the belt sander line had analyzed the data and designed a work cell on paper. The workshop schedule called for moving equipment Wednesday afternoon in order to test run the new cell on Thursday morning. At lunchtime Wednesday, the team leader and I met the plant's maintenance manager to explain the need to move the equipment and hook it up by evening so that the team could test the new process design on Thursday. The maintenance manager then commenced to explain, at some length, that moving the machines required killing the power, breaking concrete, pulling new electrical cables under the floor to the intended cell location, testing the wiring to the commercial electrical code, using a forklift to move the machines, repairing the concrete, and finally remarking the floors for safety.
>
> Ok, when could you do all that so that we can test it in production? I asked.
>
> We can't do this kind of heavy work until Christmas shutdown, he replied.
>
> On that day, it was the middle of July.
>
> I fought off my instinctive fight-flight response and stayed present in the moment. I was aware that any maintenance manager would have his crews working of projects in his annual objectives and that all are loath to disrupt them. However, he had been instructed by the plant manager to fully support the lean event that week. Christmas break was six months away. I thought to myself: That isn't going to work.

Hmm, I said, stalling for time. So, how long will it take to break the concrete and re-do the power in December?

For my full crew, a couple of days, at least! He was clearly pleased with his answer, as if that was the end of it.

I listened to his answer and calculated that two days was sixteen hours of work for his full crew which was doable during the rest of the week. And, I suspected that he was sandbagging his number. So I said:

The power is down now and we have two full days left this week, so say that your crew works here the rest of Wednesday and all day Thursday and see how it goes.

The maintenance manager groaned, turned away, called his supervisor, and told him to pull his mechanics and electricians off current projects for the rest of the week to move them over to set up the work cell.

Starting shortly after lunch, his full maintenance staff arrived and worked about nine hours disconnecting lines, moving equipment, breaking concrete, re-routing electrical lines under the floor, and testing the power at the new location. On Thursday, the team tested the new work cell as planned, and it was deemed a success. Afterward, one team member joked: Christmas came in July this year.

Lean Thinking in Knowledge Work and Services

In recent decades, productivity increases have reduced the cost of consumer goods, enabling people to spend more of their wages on services. In 1979, for example, it took 10.5 hours of an average employee's wages to buy a bicycle, but by 2015, the same worker could buy a bike with only 4 hours of income. As a result, consumer spending on services has grown dramatically in recent decades. It's estimated that the result has been that in 1950, some 40 percent of American jobs were in services, but by 2005, the share of service jobs had reached to 56 percent, and it continues to climb.[4]

As service and knowledge work organizations have grown to meet growing consumer demand, most just added staff and became ever more bureaucratic. Beginning in the 2000s, the managers in service companies began sponsoring value stream mapping and lean events to improve work effectiveness and customer service. The sketch in Figure 5.2 is my "process at a glance" for value stream mapping service and knowledge work.[5]

The Value Stream Mapping Workshop Process-at-a-Glance

1. Define the project charter and deliverables, then set up a blank map with swim lanes for each functional group involved in the process to be mapped. Mark a rough process timeline across the top.	
2. Functional groups populate the swim lanes with the tasks, decisions ◇, and work in process inventories △ they complete as part of the process. Each group uses a different color.	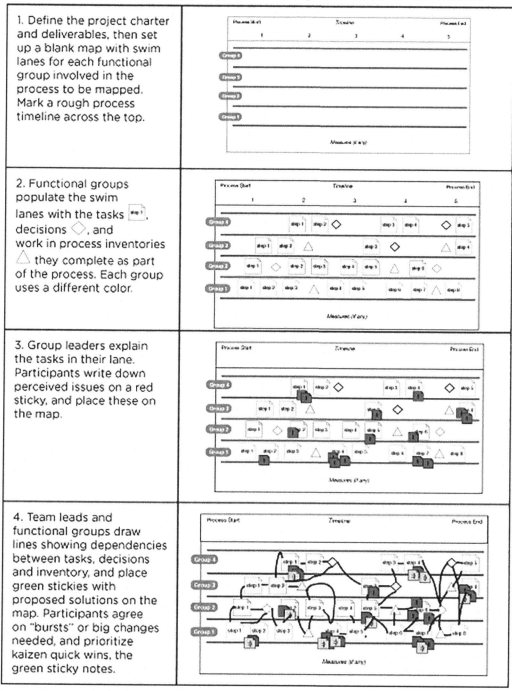
3. Group leaders explain the tasks in their lane. Participants write down perceived issues on a red sticky, and place these on the map.	
4. Team leads and functional groups draw lines showing dependencies between tasks, decisions and inventory, and place green stickies with proposed solutions on the map. Participants agree on "bursts" or big changes needed, and prioritize kaizen quick wins, the green sticky notes.	

Figure 5.2   Process at a glance for value stream mapping.

In service and knowledge work, one department's process waste and quality defects are often caused by problems rooted upstream or in a parallel department's workflow. In a value stream mapping exercise, a manager, coach, or facilitator directs each departmental team to post their current work on a wall chart within a functional "swim lane." The aim is to put everyone's workflow in public view and open up a discussion to untangle the compound and cross-functional issues that inhibit cost, quality, and delivery.

During a visioning session, author Drew Locher suggests that the team consider several questions:[6] (1) What does the customer need, in terms of future demand or production rate (takt time), the lead time or service level, and the quality performance that the new system is expected to deliver? (2) How might we apply continuous flow, pull, leveling, and lean management? (3) What waste is a significant obstacle to the defined objectives and should thus be priorized on a kaizen list?

In order to find solutions to chronic and compound problems, some that have been avoided for years, value stream mapping needs to break two corporate taboos. The first is the unspoken but well-understood rule against employees being transparent about their own department's work process waste and quality problems – the good, the bad, and the ugly. The second taboo to break the rule against declaring that one department's work or that its management policies are creating constraints or problems in another function. In order to get valid information during an improvement event, it's essential for a coach or facilitator to break these taboos. He will most likely need to "lean in" and at times push participants to be fully transparent. Once everyone is open about their work issues, the team can identify root causes and propose structure, systems, or policy solutions to big problems (called "bursts"). When big changes have been agreed-to at the appropriate level, a future state vision can be drafted and officially chartered by leadership. For example, in value stream mapping at hedge fund on Wall Street, the accounting process was back loaded and daily statements often arrived to investors late in the evening. A value stream mapping team posted the complex process on a 30-foot conference room wall. When top executives met and reviewed the big process map and saw the way to do an early valuation of customer's accounts, they approved the process change, one that had long been blocked by a power struggle between departments.

As shown in Figure 5.3, functional team leaders begin by assuming all burst improvements are successful and sketching a future workflow on a

| White Board Draft | Post-it Note Flow | Value Stream Proposal |

Figure 5.3 Drafting a value stream vision.

white board. That sketch is followed by a discussion and a consensus on the changes by all cross-functional team members. Next, the leaders reorganize the current-state post-it notes to reflect the new vision. Finally, after all team members buy-in, the draft vision is programmed into a software program for executive review and final approval.

In recent decades, health care operations managers have used value stream mapping and lean thinking to focus on improving the work.

Lean Thinking in Health Care

Due to the escalating costs of health care in recent decades, many hospitals and clinics are applying lean thinking to redesign patient flow and operations, in order to improve the quality of care. In the case below, lean coach Gary Bergmiller helped a staff on one ward apply lean thinking to their work.[7]

> A hospital management team was looking to dramatically improve the productivity of a particular ward. As a coach, I can create barriers by rigidly using tools in a lean event, or by allowing local managers to hold on to the decisions about changing the medical staff's work. Instead of over-packaging operational change tools, I tried to learn what my clients were comfortable with and go with that. When we got serious, we focused on their value stream and worked together to resolve known issues. The coaching approach is about making social connections with the employees who do the work and encouraging them to redesign the work together. During the event, I took over a former patient conference area as a war room, and I kept it simple by communicating with flip charts. We

used A3 problem-solving forms, value-stream maps, and kaizen improvements. During the week, I told the team-You are representing all employees on the unit, and I want you to collaborate with everyone. Each day, different staff members were brought in to review proposals and in-progress work changes. All teams go through the social maturation stages of forming, storming, norming, and performing. The process of forming a new team is stressful, and the coach needs to help team members communicate and stick together. It was important for me to take a parenting approach to change and help them mature as a group, that is, to help them work together like a family. When hospital staff work together to change how work gets done, they will sustain the new processes long after the coach is gone.

Applying lean thinking on a single ward is a microcosm of transforming an entire hospital or health care system.[8] Sarah Patterson, now the lean sensei at the Virginia Mason Institute, was the chief operating officer at Virginia Mason hospital at the time its leadership team first visited Toyota. As a team, they subsequently decided to adopt its lean approach as their management system in health care operations.[9] Here is her recollection of the evolution of their hospital leadership team in applying lean thinking.[10]

When we went to visit the Toyota Assembly Plant, the trip was eye-opening and a key defining moment for our leadership team. When I saw that they had designed elegant systems to protect their car doors from incurring damage during the assembly process, I said to a colleague that we needed to put as much focus and energy into designing our care processes to protect our patients from harm. During the trip our leadership team made the decision to adopt the Toyota Production System as our management approach. We told everyone: This is our management system and as a leadership team we are all in. We knew that the first thing we had to change was how we behaved as leaders. We intended to be out where the work is going on, to go-see problems and ask questions. Our job was not to be problem solvers, but problem-framers, to create the structure and accountability so that the people who did the work would also solve problems and improve the work. We also knew that we would have to rely on each other for inspiration and support during the tough times, like when there was push-back from people or when an improvement event didn't go well. Over the years we've had our nay-sayers and I've learned that conflict isn't a bad thing, it's a sign that people care. Your employees will also tell you that they are worried that you will give up because they have seen management do that before with other initiatives. Successful change requires leaders to be persistent and we learned that if we leaned-in on challenges, we could overcome them and achieve higher levels of performance.

It wasn't easy but it was incredibly rewarding to see how people responded when they realized that we were really committed to this new way of leading and that it meant better care for our patients. We continue to take trips to Toyota and what we see there continues to inspire us. It's not about the tools but about having a long-term vision, focusing on continuous improvement and never giving up. We say at Virginia Mason: Better never stops.

Many types of service enterprises are now sponsoring value stream mapping and lean events to improve their knowledge work process.

Lean Thinking in Marketing

In the 21st century, most service businesses need to offer timely bargains and communicate them to customers online. In the case below, a marketing executive sponsored a value stream mapping event aimed to redesign the process that offered on-line customers weekend deals on rental cars at airports across the United States.

The car rental company aimed to offer vacationers good deals on weekends when business rentals were slow in major cities. Marketing's challenge was to predict where excess cars would be parked at urban airports on Friday by the end of Tuesday. This number would let marketing managers target weekend offers at selected airports on Wednesday morning, which would, in turn, enable the information technology team to do the programming work, check its quality, and go live with bargain prices online by late Wednesday night or very early Thursday morning. The lean design team members were drawn from marketing, business analysis, web development, computer and server support, and testing/validation functions.

They first created a lengthy value stream map, and in reviewing it, the team realized that marketing management's slow decision making was the biggest obstacle to posting bargains on time. If the final adjustments by senior managers were late or changed after posting, they caused a churn of rework that whip-sawed downstream groups and the result was a Friday post – one that sacrificed Thursday sales to competitors.

The joint marketing-IT team defined a future state flow, planned focused work cells, and secured commitments from management for precise timing of decisions so that coding work would finish on time and offers could go live late Wednesday night.

In a follow-up phone call 2 years later, the manager described the value of the lean marketing process and the new cellular structure that supported it:[11]

> The web-development cells have grown to service all areas of our e-commerce business (customer-facing applications). However, we've had a challenge creating the ideal cross-functional cells due to fluctuating team size. At one point, a reduction in staff hurt the quality, speed and timelines of our software releases. Our subsequent inability to hire greatly hindered us as well, so we augmented each cell with consultant resources. This tactic helped us scale up our capacity and do more work than we previously thought possible. Last year we were able to release 45-plus major projects plus we launched the new product website. Even with a recent reorganization, we now seldom find bugs in production. Managers are measured by how they support the team. We have done lots of work to ensure that the cells are efficient, effective, and each team is happy working collaboratively. We discuss both successes and failures, and regularly ask the teams for input on how to improve. We are all charged up to be part of a culture of expertise and process discipline.

Some knowledge work processes, such as legal services, rely on a few internal experts who make assessments and key decisions, and as a result, their backlogs often grow even while downstream processes are starved for work.

Lean Thinking in a Law Office

Lawyers often consider legal services work to be customized to each client and as a result, aren't generally receptive to standardizing and timing their work process. In the example below, an executive sponsor set an aggressive target for reducing the total lead time and empowered attorneys and paralegals to value stream map and redesign their patent-filing process.

A new American law required inventors to file intellectual property claims much faster. In order to respond, a corporate legal director sponsored a lean event aimed to reduce the lead-time for filing from over 200 days to a future target of 120 days. After an initial orientation to process waste, the team set out to map the existing process and redesign it.

On the first day of the event, the team completed a wall-filling value stream map that included all functional work and decisions. They computed an average lead-time for filing a patent was a whopping 222 calendar days, and realized that achieving the sponsor's target would require a breakthrough redesign of their process.

On the second day, the team drafted a proposal for a parallel "fast track," one that would push less complicated ideas forward, yet didn't change the main legal workflow. In a review at the end of the day, the executive sponsor rejected the fast-track proposal as inadequate and sent the team back to the drawing board.

On day three, process data showed that there were big batches of work in process (WIP) in lawyer's dockets, going to and from the attorneys. Specifically, a clerk loaded new patent requests into the docket, a queue of work for an attorney. When the legal work was completed, finished forms were batched into a queue waiting for the analytics manager to appraise the value of each patent opportunity, and finally move it back to the attorney in control, called the responsible party or RP. They were causing what the team called "black holes" of WIP, where the patent work flow was no longer moving.

During the third day, aiming to reduce the black holes, the team proposed putting the analytics work before the attorney's review and empowering its experienced manager to triage all incoming proposals in order to determine their potential value right away. After doing his research, he was empowered to accept or reject a proposal according to its commercial value, and push only those with high potential forward and into different "lanes" depending on level of value. Lawyers then only had to assess the uniqueness of those ideas and push them forward to management in small batches for final approval.

One of the three department managers volunteered to conduct a three-month trial of the new lean patent process. During the experiment, their total lead time declined from 222 to 173 days. When counting only the new work, the lead time goal of 120 days was met 90 percent of the time (and the anomalies were being studied). Even before the trial was over, the other two department managers were clamoring for permission to adopt the new lean process.

Many financial back offices are applying value stream mapping and lean thinking to improve their responsiveness and the quality of the customer experience. Here's an example.

Lean Thinking in Banking

Prime Bank (not its real name) is an American enterprise with coast-to-coast offices that provide financial services.[12] Its corporate ATM manager worked with a lean coach to apply visual management of the value stream plus real-time data collection to enable the corporate staff to quickly respond to an anomaly at an ATM anywhere in North America through the Internet. Here is the manager's take on his company's application of lean thinking that enabled empowered team problem solving.[13]

> Our customer is much more demanding now, and our response time is critical to beating the competition. We can't allow lost time in transactional processing at a branch in our division. So we are building a universal approach to "here and now" problem solving in the value flow of ATM transactions. What is interesting is that because we are a back-office function that's one step removed from end customers, our employees weren't previously able to recognize customer issues and respond to them quickly.
>
> We hire people who are phenomenal problem solvers in general, but they may not always understand the customer outcome the company needs. One of my "aha" realizations has been that it

takes a lot more work to teach them to do problem solving than I thought it would. I repeatedly take individuals to the visual board showing our value stream flow and ask them to describe the end value to customers in their own words. It took a lot of effort to get a group of 40–50 people to understand why they are here, to be able to see customer value, to be real-time problem solvers and for them to adopt this new way to do their work. I often gave them an opportunity to openly criticize any aspect of our problem-solving process, and 85 percent of them viewed the visual management and coaching as valuable.

I'm doing three things to empower my staff in problem solving. One thing is to making sure we agree on the outcomes that our service value chain is driving; the second thing is enabling problem solving in real time; and the third is determining how the company should invest in improving those outcomes in the future. We're playing the long game not the short game here. In the long game, developing problem-solving capability in the ATM team is essential.

Since our staff received coaching and now understands our customer, they have been consciously addressing the customer's ATM experience and resolving arising problems in our value stream quickly. As a result, I now feel a lot more confident that we are upping the collective level of problem solving in our division. I go to the floor frequently, and I operate with a high degree of confidence in the team. Even if I were hit by a bus today, after my funeral tomorrow they could go into problem solving automatically and get us out of anomalies at any ATM natiionwide.

A company's disjointed product development process can plant seeds for all kinds of operational problems, cost issues, and quality defects downstream. That makes it a prime target for the application of value stream mapping and lean thinking.

Lean Thinking in Product Development

Coauthors James M. Morgan and Jeffrey K. Liker have described the concepts of lean product and process development this way:[14] (1) understand customers and their context in order to create the right product;

(2) develop process excellence in order to deliver with speed and precision and achieve a mix of fixed and flexible operations; (3) develop high-performing teams, team members, and product development leaders; (4) capture and apply know-how; and (5) pursue product perfection. The value of lean product and process development can be a reduction of downstream costs, higher product quality, and a halo effect for a company and its products.

There are two mutually reinforcing approaches to creating flow in development: Building flow into the process at the start and helping your team synchronize work in real time.[15] Building flow into the process ensures the development team makes the most of incomplete but stable information and enables concurrency.

To build flow into the process, first design the development tasks and their sequence to maximize the utility of vital inputs and outputs. Then determine milestones and schedule integration events when teams can coordinate and evaluate progress based on agreed-upon quality-of-event criteria. To help this evaluation, be sure to use input requirements as leading indicators of progress. Value stream and decision mapping are often reasonable ways to start your development process re-design.

Unfortunately, no process, no matter how well designed, will be sufficient. Organizing and leading your development team to synchronize work in real time during development helps the team respond to inevitable unexpected situations. As Mike Tyson says, "everyone has a plan until they get punched in the face." Stuff happens. Things go wrong. Teams need to be able to react and keep making progress in the face of unexpected changes. Effective obeya stand-up meetings and good visual management are very helpful here, and a strong chief engineer leading the program is essential. Depending on the product, you may want to consider organizing cross-functional teams around product sub-systems. The point is that you need tools and mechanisms that give the team an early heads-up and enable them to absorb inevitable variation and keep moving forward.

Dr. Morgan summarizes lean product development this way: "Lean development is more about developing a shared understanding of the work to be done and increasing fidelity as you close gaps over time."[16] He continues: "It happens by enabling skilled and talented people to work together persistently and collaboratively to create something seemingly impossible."[17] Where can talented people collaborate and get coaching for lean process and product development?

Product Development Obeya

A product development "obeya", meaning "big room" in Japanese, is a dedicated space and a visual system intended to accelerate the development of new products and processes by making work visible and increasing cross-functional collaboration. During weekly or biweekly stand-up meetings in an obeya, each functional team shares status information, asks and answers questions, coordinates decisions across all functions, identifies problems to be solved off-line, clarifies the functions responsible for decisions and solutions, and holds all involved accountable to fulfill their commitments to a team's product development plan and schedule. A sketch of a typical obeya room is shown in Figure 5.4.

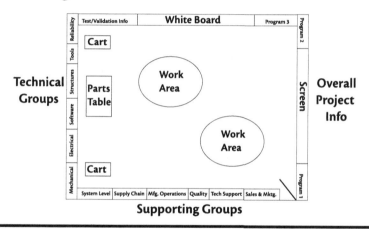

Figure 5.4 Obeya room layout.

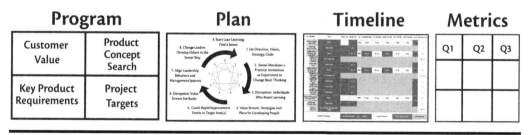

Figure 5.5 Program visual.

While each product development team's project journey will be somewhat unique, some common elements can help an obeya process become a productive ritual.

The program visual sketched in Figure 5.5 is a wall posting in an obeya that shares information on an overall development program. It includes reference information on customer value, key product requirements, a product concept, and high-level targets.[18] In addition to program information, departmental leads post subsystem and function information in an obeya.

As shown in Figure 5.6, subsystem and functional product development teams highlight "need to know" information and "need to share" information with others. They visually post performance attributes for technical performance and describe "glide path" activities intended to reach each one.[19] Product development teams often meet once or twice a week in a stand-up meeting in an obeya, and some meet there in a morning "huddle" every day.

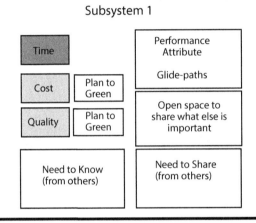

Figure 5.6   Subsystem or function visual.

As work progresses through different phases of product development, the content on the obeya walls should change accordingly. Lean coach Katrina Appell writes that a good obeya physical setup and meeting process helps people: (1) Make decisions relatively quickly with technical experts discussing trade-offs; (2) get team alignment on what the product needs to be; (3) enable cross-functional integration and collaboration; (4) identify problems early; and (5) facilitate cross-functional problem solving.[20] In the obeya meeting, each functional team reviews their work in progress, and all others can post new red notes as Andon signals for potential problems. As functional team members share issues, their openness creates coaching opportunities for product development managers. Dr. John Drogosz describes typical tasks and obstacles that design teams may encounter and need to overcome:

■ Find a space: In the beginning, many organizations face the fundamental challenge of finding a space for an obeya. Many say, "We already have enough problems finding a conference room for meetings, and now you want to dedicate a room for just one project?" In some instances, it may take some creativity to find a suitable location. Look for open areas that can be enclosed with temporary walls, like a space in the corner of the prototype shop, or double-up people in one office in order to free up a room. If there is a will, a solution will present itself.

■ Take the time to stop and set up the space: The initial setup of the obeya is a team sport. It will take a half to a whole day, but setting up is the first demonstration by team members that they are committed to trying to work in an obeya. In fact, it is a great team-building exercise for a project kickoff.

■ Decide what's most relevant or useful: Creating meaningful visuals is easier said than done. Initially, team members are uncertain about what to track and display. In the beginning, they will frequently overdo it and post way more information than they or their team needs. Not to worry – as the team continues to work in an obeya, the visuals that are most value-added will become apparent, and the others will gradually fade away. Similarly, in the beginning, obeya meetings will take more time, but as teams practice their routines, the discussions will become more focused. Before this happens, the team needs to go through a phase of experimentation and learning.

Setting up an obeya shouldn't be a massive undertaking. In the case below, Dr. Drogosz describes how one design team successfully set up an obeya.[21]

One company starting an obeya was a large manufacturer of industrial equipment with multiple divisions serving customers in several countries. The company group interested was designing the next-generation product for one of their key product lines. The leadership of the division saw the need to accelerate their time-to-market to meet their competition.

The project team for the product saw a sizable challenge in front of them from both a technical and a timing perspective. However, when their project manager first proposed the idea of stating an obeya, one member of the team was skeptical, saying: We already have all that information on-line that everyone can access, we already have too many meetings. Another said: Our team is spread out all over the place, so why have a central physical space? A third member said: We have had war rooms in the past for key projects, but they turned out to be dog-and-pony shows for senior managers.

So the first step in convincing them to do an obeya was to identify the problems they might solve there, that an obeya would help the team be successful. Leadership had given them the challenge to reduce their new product's time-to-market by at least 25 percent, and in a follow-on team meeting, they identified a number of obstacles to achieving that goal. One of the most crucial was the need to improve cross-functional collaboration to enable faster development times. As the discussion proceeded, they became more willing to consider an obeya as a potential solution.

There's no one best way to set up an obeya. Initially, team members are often uncertain about what to display. In the beginning, the team spent half a day designing and installing an initial set of visual aids. They posted more information than they later deemed as needed. The project leaders used the obeya setup during the project kickoff as a team-building exercise. They conducted their first stand-up meeting to pilot-test the activity and give feedback to their peers on their first drafts of visuals on the wall. As the group continued to work over the initial weeks, the most useful visuals became apparent and some not-so-good ones were taken down.

Since design team members expected product development to be "lean," they wanted to spend less time in meetings, not more. Yet in the beginning, their obeya meetings took more time than planned. Team members debated the usefulness of various visuals – which ones worked, which ones did not, and they struggled with how much detail to share. Initially, some meetings were too status-oriented, and in others, people got sidetracked into problem solving during the meeting itself. They found the obeya sessions challenging in the first month, as they were learning new ways to interact, yet they still needed to get the actual project work done.

In those early stages, the executive sponsor was concerned about keeping the team engaged and working together. He considered a key to be having a strong project manager, one who was patient and had the perseverance to keep improving the obeya process. In the first couple of months, the team built-in a 10-minute reflection at the end of every other obeya meeting.

They reviewed how they were using the space and how the meeting rituals were working, and then agree on what needed to be improved or jettisoned. In addition, the lean coach was essential for giving ongoing guidance and feedback to the project manager and the team in the treacherous early stages of meeting in the obeya. As the team learned to improve their meeting rituals, discussions gradually became more focused and the meeting time dropped from 90-plus minutes once a week to between 20 and 30 minutes twice a week.

Over time, the team adopted an Andon color-coded system that made both technical and business issues visible. As each function became comfortable asking for assistance from others, each received immediate help, and was then able to make progress at an accelerated pace. At one point, a team member evaluated her project's obeya room experience this way: When people meet in the obeya, it helps them stay on the same page and they see the bigger picture of how their work fits in and how they can help others.

The team was ultimately able to launch the next-generation product in 30 percent less time with the same number of people, and there were many fewer production preparation issues late in development. In the end, the team viewed the obeya as one of the major contributors to their success.

Why Are Lean Startups So Difficult to Sustain and Spread?

In his book, *Flow Manufacturing*, author Richard J. Schonberger summarized his consulting visits to 101 companies. While touring their factories to review operations, he found that many were struggling to sustain the initial promise of their past lean startups. Here's his view of the current state of lean operations in many companies.[22]

Lean manufacturing/lean management has been faring poorly. Many-year up-down inventory cycles are a concrete indicator, and one that shows a disturbing down (worsening) cycle dating through the 2000s. Paralleling the hard-data inventory evidence are tendencies of companies to rely more on "soft" practices while

paying less attention to methodologies that actually change processes for the better (cells, quick set-up, etc.)

It has long been a theory that a so-called lean "model line" would spontaneously spin off by motivating other operations managers to start similar
"daughter" lean lines across a facility (Figure 5.7).

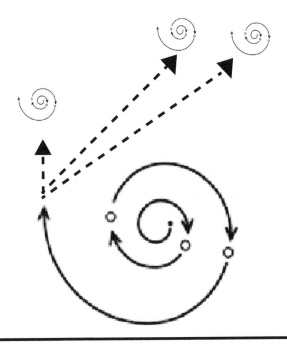

Figure 5.7   Spontaneous spin-offs.

However, author James P. Womack has toured many companies, and he
notes that:[23]

> I have often found in my company visits that the model line never
> spreads from the original example and that in many cases, the
> model itself regressed, with the progressive addition of inventories
> between steps and even deconstruction to isolated villages.

Unfortunately, despite peoples' initial enthusiasm for a lean model line, and
their great potential demonstrated early on, neither their work designs nor
their team collaboration seems to be easily sustained or readily spread to other
work areas. In fact, most change leaders, coaches, and experts estimate that
somewhere between 1 and 10 percent of new lean startups are able to sustain their initial scope or potential beyond a few weeks or months. Successful

startups seem to be limited to "sweet spots," that is, processes where managers and employees were always receptive to try the next improvement – hardly the constraint operations most in need of transformation. And when new lean startups fail to sustain their initial gains, some managers resort to soft practices like team management or servant leadership, which may well not get to the root problem of a failing lean process. Below are a few of the numerous obstacles that prevent success or stop the spread of successful models:

- Pushing changes without enough orientation and involvement of employees.
- Having limited technical resource capacity to support kaizen and systems improvements.
- Attempting multiple, concurrent change efforts of various types that overload or confuse employees.
- Failing to win buy-in from middle managers who view changes as the flavor of the month.
- Using a reengineering approach to force-fit lean work methods.
- Insufficient "socializing" of the future-state vision, the plan for change, and the impact of the change on employee's job security and quality of work life.
- Politicking against change by union officials or informal shop-floor leaders.
- Employee distrust fueled by past disappointments with management or change programs.
- Support systems fail to serve the new needs of lean startups.
- Supportive managers are transferred before lean changes are stabilized.
- Enthusiastic but inexperienced managers try lean methods on an unstable process.
- Failing to gain full commitment among site or business leadership team members.
- Middle managers prioritize their "silo" work over sustaining new learn startups.

Despite such hindrances and others unique to a business, when a sponsoring executive and all members of a business or site leadership team buy-in to a lean vision and its complimentary leadership approach, they will eventually generate a high degree of success. Business executive and author George Koenigsaecker described one of his successful lean implementations this way:[24]

Over two-plus years, our company redesigned its lines as focused factories or value streams, taking each of them to a new level of performance. Overall, we were able to take our lead times down from more than thirty days to one day, with 100 percent on-time delivery, and we reduced quality issues by over 80 percent. Best of all, we grew enterprise productivity by 86 percent, which was right at our 2 percent per month target. As we gained traction, our group executive began to spread the system to the other companies in his group, and it became known as our business system.

One common problem happens when managers become distracted by what's called the "shiny-object syndrome." Here's an example from Frank Giannattasio, the former vice president of operations at Wiremold (Legrand's North American operations) and now a consultant for "Lean Ideas."[25]

One of my biggest clients was a chemical company. In one of their lines, there was a spray-drier that operated at 1,800 degrees. When a machine changeover was scheduled, it had to cool down, be thoroughly cleaned, and then reheated before the introduction of new chemicals. The unaided cool-down took up to 12 hours. During the kaizen event, the team made several improvements that resulted in time reductions and cleaned the downstream process. They also found a way to pull the drier out of its cylinder or "sleeve" so it could cool much faster in the ambient air. Out of the sleeve, it would take only five hours to cool, freeing up lots of production capacity. The changeover improvement would require the purchase of a crane to extract the sleeve, but the ROI was high and plant management agreed to fund it. Yet by the time of my return visit the following month, everything had changed. When I arrived on a Monday morning, the plant's lean facilitator met me in the conference room and said that management had lost the commitment to purchase the new crane, and that all the managers felt they were too busy to discuss it. One had gone to Europe, and the others said they had other things to do. They paid me just to walk around the factory all week.

Perhaps the biggest reason why many lean startups don't deliver on their initial promise is that few operating managers who become "foster parents" so to speak, of lean processes, understand their new "child". They don't realize that a lean operation isn't "something to do" but rather is all about "something to learn."

A Lean Operation Is a Learning Organization

Author Peter Senge has written that a learning organization is: "A collage of activities, new governing ideas, innovations in infrastructure, and new management tools for changing ways people conduct their work."[26] However, in a lean operation, the continuous learning isn't about a collage of things; rather, employees are to continuously learn better ways to solve problems, improve quality, and redesign the work itself. Here's the testimony of one lean product development coach who was surprised to learn that lean product development wasn't a hard and fast set of ideas, infrastructure, or tools.[27]

> When I began learning about the Toyota system, our consultants told me that the lean approach was to be a learning organization. Actually, I was expecting something more striking. But when we began value-stream mapping our product development process, I saw lots of red sticky notes that indicated a lot of problems that we could solve. We had previously solved product development problems one by one with the 5-Why analysis. However, on our lean journey we learned what I call the sixth why, and it was often the root cause that led engineers to abandon a lean change.
>
> Digging down to the sixth "why," we found that our company's cultural values didn't support the standard work required to capture the gains from our value stream mapping and problem solving. What was the issue? I sometimes say: Old guys won't read a book. That is, our development engineers didn't want to follow new improved standards for doing the work. It won't ever last if you don't change the technical culture to one that values learning and standardization. After the first four or five years of applying lean thinking in my company, most of the gains had disappeared. But

recently, things changed a bit. I was getting lots of phone calls and being bombarded with priority meetings because engineers trying to accelerate projects even when their priorities or scope had been changed. I asked myself: How can I help them see that the biggest pain in their day is the result of pushing work forward too fast? In a redesign session we applied lean thinking to set up a pull process for their design work. They now understand that a pull process reduces the waste of non-value added discussions. Once we got beyond the meeting issue, I finally succeeded in getting engineers to ask: Why do we work the way we currently do, and how could we do it better? If you get that point as a company, you're in great shape.

When managers don't understand that a lean operation is a learning organization, they fail to provide a climate of respect which enables employees' learning to start and strengthen over time.

Respect for People

Rather than managers leading the startup of lean tools and systems, a lean organization is more about the involvement of everyone in an ongoing science experiment. And in order for people to take the risks necessary to experiment, fail, and learn, they need to feel safe and respected by a coach or manager. Lean coaches Mike Orzen and David Verble describe the conditions necessary to establish a learning organization:[28]

> Our human need to feel connected and accepted is being met. This makes it much more likely that we will feel safe exercising our discretionary effort and willingly take responsibility for contributing and making things better.

Leaders need to respect all employees, even those who resist change because it is essential to sustaining learning and redesigning work processes. Here's an example:

> I was leading a lean event in a factory machining area one week. The union steward in the area was not receptive to either the Japanese idea of kaizen or to outside consultants. Like many in his

union, he saw the lean events as just ways to get more work out of union workers for free. He dutifully attended the opening orientation on the first morning of the lean event but refused to join the kaizen team. After the kick-off, he returned to the security of his nearby office. But even though he was listed as a participant the workshop, I let him slide. I saw him periodically as I walked along a hallway and looked through his office window. He was often on the phone or meeting one-on-one with employees. I was aware that the steward was opting out, but I continued to show respect for him. Part of a union steward's job is to defend his member's rights, and I knew little of the terms of the contract or the specifics the union's role in the plant.

Later the first day, I knocked on his office door and he invited me in. We chatted a bit about his work history and about his perceptions of plant operations. I listened patiently to his skeptical questions and doubts. I let go of my need to convince him to attend the event and chatted with him personally and authentically. I briefed him on the upcoming tasks for day two, telling him that we would start with a clean-up program called 5S. I told him that we would remove unneeded equipment, clean the area thoroughly, standardize locations for materials, machines and tools, and then move on redesigning the work process the following day. He listened to my spiel, leaned back in his chair for a couple of moments, and then said: That's fine, but could you get management to buy some new mats and place them in front of the machines where our workers have to stand for hours on end? I said that I'd check into it. Out in machining, I examined the floor mats and saw that they indeed were thin and had holes in them. Since I was authorized to buy needed supplies, I asked the plant's purchasing manager to order new mats with expedited delivery. As the 5S work continued, the new mats arrived in the afternoon and were placed on the newly clean floors in front of each grinding machine. At the end of the day, I noticed the union steward walking through the area and checking out the new mats.

The next morning, I knocked on his office door early and he invited me in a second time. I asked him to join in on the kaizen work that day, telling him that we would begin by listing waste or known problems and then brainstorm ideas to improve the work on the newly-clean line. We would prioritize and combine the team's ideas and test them if possible, and then sketch a future-state workflow on a whiteboard. Once a new layout was reviewed and approved by the operations managers, we would help maintenance move equipment into the new configuration, and if feasible, test it out. He was noncommittal. Yet a little later, and with no fanfare, he joined the team and soon became just as motivated as the other team members. Showing respect for him, despite his resistance to change, paid off for the company, the employees, and for me as the coach.

Why is respect so important? Lean thinking must be embedded in a community, one with norms of respect, reason, teamwork and creativity. They are formed when individuals step up and face conflict within their team and with their management – something that never gets easy. It can and should be assisted by leaders and coaches who facilitate resolution when differences arise on a team.

A lean team culture is one with norms that support standardization and discipline, and taboos for poor performance. Decades ago social science research discovered that cohesive communities form through a standard social process of forming, storming, norming and performing. If those steps are avoided due to fear, or obstructed by a few with social status, lean teams will revert to their prior bureaucratic thinking and level of performance.

Reflection: What Can We Learn from Lean Thinking?

The early and ready success of lean events gave executives, plant managers, and operations managers the misimpression that they could transform their traditional business into a lean operation in a few months or a couple of years.[29] So in past decades, they often mapped their value streams and pushed lean methods out onto their shop floors. In so doing, they treated employees as mere scientific abstractions. Naturally when employees felt objectified as inert "parts" of a system, few were motivated enough to deliver the disciplined effort that sustains new lean workflows. They lost their kaizen minds. So just how can a company engage its employees in a way that motivates them to sustain the gains of new lean work? Lean coaching is the third key to transforming a Western business into a lean operation.

What You Can Do

Form a cadre of managers and coaches to share their ongoing learning about leading change to a lean enterprise. Download my value stream mapping at a glance for service and knowledge work, and begin lean events with receptive teams.[30] If past lean work startups are fading to mass production or management is snapping back to command and control, do a "5 why" analysis. Then, when the time is right, elevate the cadre's assessment of constraints and root causes of the setbacks to higher management for discussion and set a new strategy for lasting lean success.

Notes

1 *Zen and Creative Management*, Albert Low, Charles E. Tuttle Company, 1976, p. xvii.
2 Comment by an American executive who is to remain anonymous.
3 *Journey to Lean*, John Drew, Blair McCallum, and Stefan Roggenhofer, Palgrave McMillan, 2004, p. 36–45
4 A 2013 analysis by David Author and David Dorn, cited in The Jobs Americans Do, by Benjamin Appelbaum, the New York Times Magazine, February 23, 2017.
5 https://blog.lucidmeetings.com/hubfs/facilitator-guides/Value-Stream-Mapping-Facilitators-Guide.pdf.
6 *What Too Many Value-Stream Maps Completely Miss*, Drew Locher, LEI Lean Post, March 8, 2016.
7 Gary Bergmiller interview in San Francisco, 2015.
8 On their website, the Virginia Mason System including 336 beds, over 500 doctors, and 5,500 employees.
9 See *Transforming Health Care: Virginia Mason Medical Center's Pursuit of the Perfect Patient Experience*, Charles Kenny, Productivity Press, 2011.
10 Sarah Patterson, MHA, FACMPE, is the executive director of Virginia Mason Institute. She presented at the Association of Manufacturing Excellence, 2013, Toronto, Ontario, Canada.
11 Company identity and manager remain anonymous.
12 Actual name withheld.
13 Prime Bank interview in April 2012; Review the Customer-back coaching at One System One Voice.com.
14 *Designing the Future*, James M. Morgan and Jeffrey K. Liker, McGraw-Hill, 2019, p. 5.
15 *How Synchronizing Workflows Eliminates Waste in Development Processes*, Jim Morgan, Lean Enterprise Post, LEI.org, June 25, 2021.

16 Use Lean Development Principles to avoid "Traveling Hopefully" down the Wong Path, James Morgan Lean Post, LEI.org, September 26, 2018.

17 *Designing the Future*, James M. Morgan and Jeffrey K. Liker, McGraw-Hill, 2019, p. 2.

18 According to John Drogosz, the term "search" should read "sketch."

19 Katrina Appell of the Lean Enterprise Institute contributed this function and systems chart and information.

20 *Virtual Obeya Layout*, Katrina Appell, The Lean Post, LEI.org, April 9, 2020.

21 Interview with John Drogosz, Vice President of Optiprise consulting.

22 *Assessing the State of Lean*, Richard J. Schonberger, Target Magazine, Fall 2019, p. 26–31.

23 *Rethinking the Model Line*, James P. Womack, Lean Enterprise Institute, The Lean Post, April 19, 2018.

24 *Leading the Lean Enterprise Transformation*, Second Edition, George Koenigsaecker, CRC Press, Taylor & Francis Group, a Productivity Press Book, 2013, p. 6.

25 Interview with Frank Giannattasio, Lean Ideas Consulting, in 2005.

26 *The Dance of Change, Peter Senge*, Art Kleiner, Charlotte Roberts, Richard Ross, George Roth, and Brian Smith, Currency Doubleday, 1999, p. 33.

27 Presentation at an Association for Manufacturing Excellence Conference in San Diego, CA, October 30, 2018.

28 *Show Respect, Psychological Safety, and Social Neuroscience*, Mike Orzen and David Verble, April 26, 2019.

29 *Lean Thinking*, James T. Womack and Daniel T. Jones, Simon and Schuster, 1996, p. 265.

30 https://blog.lucidmeetings.com/hubfs/facilitator-guides/Value-Stream-Mapping-Facilitators-Guide.pdf.

Chapter 6

The Third Key Is Lean Coaching

Although they wrote whole books describing specific techniques and a few high-level philosophic reflections, the thought process needed to tie all the methods into a complete system was left largely implicit.[1]

James P. Womack

Men one and all value the part of knowledge which is known. They do not know how to avail themselves of the unknown in order to reach knowledge. Is this not misguided?[2]

Chuang Tzu

IN THE TENNESSEE PLANT

Aftermarket suppliers were taking sales on specialty wheel orders by promising faster delivery. Ross, the operations manager, aimed to change that. During a lean event, he aimed to coach the wheel production work team with a PDCA cycle and Socratic questions.

Wally was the irascible leader of the wheel line, and at times, he could be highly critical of management. Yet Ross respected him, and he had privately asked him to lead the kaizen team beforehand, and Wally had agreed to do it. Despite that, at the beginning of the working session, He complained loudly about a bunch of past issues, and Ross patiently heard him out. He knew that Wally's temper rose like thunderheads in the Summer sky and would blow through as quickly a southern thunderstorm. And it did.

After a brief orientation to the eight kinds of process waste, Ross sent the team out to observe the work area as it was being run by second-shift employees. In pairs, they listed process wastes and known problems on a clipboard. When they returned to the conference room, he asked them discuss and prioritize their items on a collective list. A few of their waste items were: waiting for materials, known defects that randomly reoccurred, ergonomic problems due to an awkward machine layout, long part change over times, and others. Next, they brainstormed improvement ideas to reduce each priority waste. When a team member became excited about a specific improvement idea, Ross never shot him down. Instead, he asked lots of questions or went out to the shop floor with him to see how the proposed change might work. For instance, one idea was to relocate the grinding machines closer and rotate them from a 180-degree angle to a 90-degree, thus improving ergonomics and enabling one operator to readily run two machines. Another item on the list was waiting for one machine to finish a run so that the second one could use the same set of tooling. One employee remembered that some old tooling had been stored in a back room some years before. When he retrieved it, the team found that it was the right size and usable enough to enable two machines to run the most popular sized wheels concurrently. Two team members built a plywood board for hanging hand tools, painted it, and located tools and fixtures closer to the machines. Others worked with the scheduling department to plan more frequent delivery of baskets of raw parts and defined a pull signal to trigger each new basket. They reoriented the forklift parking angles so that the driver could unload raw parts and depart with less effort. Following the lean event, the company promised to deliver a specialty order within two weeks, and if a delivery was later, the company promised to make it free. A few months later, after online ordering and scheduling software were installed, the company promised to deliver an order within three days.

The next problem to solve in starting and sustaining a lean operation in a Western enterprise arises when impatient managers or lean coaches do value stream mapping or apply lean methods in a cold and analytical way. In so doing, they objectify employees as mere "parts" of a troublesome system, and their disrespected employees aren't motivated enough to sustain lean work processes, at least not for long. How can managers implement lean thinking in a way that motivates employees to sustain the gains? The third key to leading a lean business transformation is lean coaching. Its four aspects are shown in the table below.

Problem to Solve	Key	What Leaders Do	Leadership Challenge
Analysis objectifies and demotivates employees	Lean coaching	Coach with PDCA, a purpose and mindfulness	Enable others to act

The Three Deliberate Practices of Lean Coaching

Lean coaches create the conditions for managers, supervisors, job performers, and specialists to apply their mindfulness and creativity, their kaizen minds to redesign the work of a business operation. Figure 6.1 shows the three deliberate practices of lean coaching.

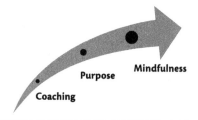

Figure 6.1   The three deliberate practices of lean coaching.

When the early Japanese sensei led kaizen events in American and European factories, their leadership philosophy and coaching approach were on full display. They followed a Zen learning approach in teaching us: they threw us in over our heads; expected us to solve real problems; provided no ready answers; and expected us to become mindful of the process in detail. In so doing, they taught us to drop our urge for quick solution ideas and instead identify waste and tap our innate creativity to reduce it. In other words, they developed our kaizen minds. The first deliberate practice of lean coaching is often using the Deming model, that is, the cycle of plan–do–check–adjust or PDCA (sometimes noted as SDCA for

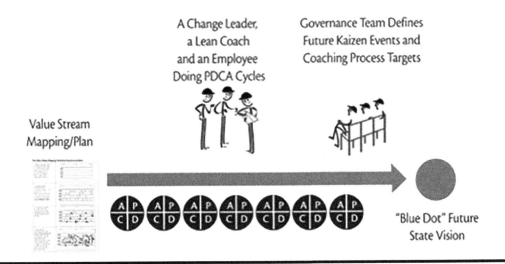

Figure 6.2 PDCA cycles progress toward a vision. Leapers © Copyright, *Lean Enterprise Institute, Inc.*, All rights reserved. Lean Enterprise Institute, the leaper image, and stick figure image are registered trademarks of *Lean Enterprise Institute, Inc.*, Used with permission.

study–do–check–adjust). Figure 6.2 pictures leaders, coaches, and employees working together to implement a long series of PDCA cycles that move an operation toward a "blue dot" or ideal future-state vision.

The Autoliv company[3] recently reported that it shipped about 700,000 air bags a week, some 40 percent of the world market, and its annual sales had zoomed past $1 billion. Its America's Division was an early adopter of lean thinking and recently wrote that it had 135 production cells and was making room for more. Mike Ward, Autoliv America's president during the company's first, unsuccessful attempt to implement Toyota's production methods[4], described the company's early early effort this way: "For the first one and a half years of lean, we used a re-engineering concept and the theory of constraints set up our production lines as u-shaped cells. Then, we in management immediately created lean teams and cut staff, and soon costs fell by 50 percent overall. But it didn't last."

Tom Hartman is a former President of Autoliv Inflators, and he recently described how the Utah, USA operation learned to coach lean:[5]

> When I joined Autoliv, we were the largest supplier to Toyota and they knew that our delivery and quality stunk, and they were either going to fix us or cut us lose, so their executives asked us this question: If we send you a teacher, will you be good students? We enthusiastically said: Yes! Subsequently, Sensei Takashi Harada

worked with us full-time for three years. However, when Mr. Harada came to our plant in Utah, none of us had told our CEO that we had agreed to have him in-house for 3 years. When he once saw him he asked me: Who is the Japanese guy, is he stealing our technology? No, I said, he's teaching us how to manage the operation and drive out waste.

Jim Bickerstaff was the first Autoliv supervisor to work with the new Japanese sensei. Mr. Harada quickly challenged his assumptions about how to run a lean production line. Here are Jim's recollections from that time.[6]

When they first asked me to work with Mr. Harada, I had no concept of what it would be like. The only reference I had about dealing with Japanese culture was seeing the movie Gung Ho,[7] which was in theaters at the time. I was afraid he'd be very, very strict like the Japanese managers in the movie. However, the guy had a great sense of humor and he was a great teacher. Luckily, I had said I would work with him. Mr. Harada taught me by asking questions, and for pretty much the whole time I worked with him, I never understood a single question. For example, we shipped a lot of GM products and had to relabel them the day they shipped with current information, such as which dock at the GM factory would take delivery. First thing every morning, we printed new labels at the first work station. It was automatic, and while employees were picking parts, some of the labels would spiral off the machine onto the floor. Seeing a stack of labels on the floor, Mr. Harada looked at me and asked,
Cat job, dog job?
Cat job! I said.
Very good, Mr. Harada said as he walked away.
I chased him across the shop floor and asked, Mr. Harada, what was that about?
He said that the Toyota production system is all about respecting humanity, and expecting people to pick up all those labels and sort them is disrespectful of employees. What he meant was that either answer I gave was OK, as long as I didn't say that picking up labels was a human job.
I met with Mr. Harada every Tuesday for half an hour, and once he wrote a comment on a whiteboard that said:
Jim-san, sometimes people need sugar, and sometimes they need salt. Jim-san, you need a lot of salt.

Noticing my look of confusion, he asked me: Isn't that English?

Yes, I said, but I have no idea what it means.

He would sometimes leave me with the question. That time I think he wrote it down because I questioned everything and often seemed confused, so sweet feedback wasn't likely to break through to me.

Another time, he taught me how to figure out the takt-time for the daily pace of production for my line. He wrote the calculation on a whiteboard and then he just left. Later, he came back and asked me:

Jim-san, what is your takt-time?

Mr. Harada, I need a part in that box every 28 seconds, I said.

Now, you can figure out how many people you need, he said.

Thinking in the old way, I said, I have 10 work stations, so I need 10 people.

No, he replied. Give each person 28 seconds-worth of work.

Following his instruction, I broke down the tasks in each job and discovered that I only needed 8 people to run the line, not 10. But part of our company's deal to get Toyota to help us was that we agreed not to lay people off as a result of improvements. Our company was growing at that time, so I sent two of my employees to work elsewhere in the factory. We set up the line with the takt-time speed synchronized to eight people, standardized the jobs at that pace, and it worked well. A short time later, Mr. Harada came to my line and asked,

Jim-san, what if your takt-time dropped to 26 seconds? Can you make everyone work harder?

I was silent because I knew he didn't want me to say yes, as it would be disrespectful to the employees.

He then asked me, Jim-san, can you change time?

No, Mr. Harada, I didn't wake up this morning as a superhero who could change time. I smiled at my joke, but he didn't, he just continued:

Yes, you can. Time is only the shadow of motion. If you bring that material closer to the worker, there is less walking. If you locate the component wires closer, you reduce time in assembly.

By changing motion, you change time. If you reduce motion, you save time. Moving equipment or changing tools is expensive and time-consuming. Motion kaizen is cheaper than machine kaizen.

The first question I asked myself from then on was, How can I change motion? Another thing Mr. Harada taught me about was one-piece flow. He asked me one day:

Jim-san, you don't run one-piece flow?

No, I said flatly. Mr. Harada, I don't believe in one-piece flow.

Jim-san, can you try one-piece flow? He asked.

Since I had agreed to work with him, I agreed to experiment with one-piece flow on my line for a week. Our first workstation in the line was often down because the barcode label station couldn't keep the labels straight. When the roll slipped, its diameter decreased, and the labels fell off the stand, so we stacked off the good ones to poles at the side of the machine. However, while that first machine was down, it didn't create a problem running the rest of the line. The line was so fast that we could work off the inventory on the poles to cover all the downtime.

When I tried one-piece flow, the workstation that made the labels was frequently down, which then meant that the rest of the line went down too. So, my team had to work the following weekend to make up for the lost production due to downtime. When Mr. Harada arrived the next Monday morning, I was ready for him and I said:

Mr. Harada, I've never had to work a weekend before to make shipments. I told you one-piece flow wouldn't work.

One-piece flow worked perfectly, he countered, it showed you where your problem is on your line.

I had been ready to go back to the old way, but as I walked away I understood his point. I muttered to myself,

Shoot, he's right again.

Mr. Harada never once told me what to do, but I was always busy because he asked the right questions. The solutions I came up with were better than having someone telling me what to do, and when they worked I stuck to them. "During his three years with us, he never answered a single one of my questions.

After Mr. Harada's three years at Autoliv, the Americas Division embraced Toyota's approach of lean coaching. At one point, the company reported having 135 production cells and was making room for more.[8] The company subsequently cited a 23 percent increase in productivity and an 88 percent reduction in defective parts in its lean operations. Their suppliers' delivery metric was up to 98.9 percent on-time, and they reported that incoming

Figure 6.3 Synchronizing doing and coaching.

supplier defects were reduced by 61 percent. The company earned awards from all of its major vehicle manufacturing customers and won the Shingo Prize for Excellence in Manufacturing at 7 of its 12 manufacturing facilities in the United States and Mexico.

In practice, a lean coach's PDCA wheel gets a spin and often starts with a "check" of facts and data in a target operation. The sketch in Figure 6.3 shows "doing" and "coaching" as two gears, and as they turn toward each other, they roughly match up the three disciplined practices of "coaching" with the four steps of "doing" beginning with the "check," that is, CAP-Do. As the gears turn, mindfulness lands between "check" and "adjust" and covers both, enabling awareness to check for new facts and data, plus adjust a job performer's or team's past understanding of the situation and identify a root cause, the problem to solve. Continuing to rotate, the coach's practice of purpose lands between "adjust" and "plan" and covers both. So a coach helps a job performer or team translate a root cause into a "purpose." Finally, the coach applies a practice of "coaching" to help a job performer or team to both detail the plan and "do" an experiment to test a potential solution. Then, after finishing an implementation or experiment, a new cycle of CAP-Do begins.

In the case below, I coached a product development manager, Colin, who was planning a working meeting with his company's internal software leads. His goal was to get them set up sufficient budget to deliver his version 2.0 machine software requirements the following year. Before our meeting began, I had been away on vacation, so I started with a bit of schmoozing, which is always a good idea.

Check and Adjust – Be Mindful of Change and Make Adjustments
Hi Colin, I'm back from my vacation, so let's discuss the upcoming 2.0 software workshop. I think I've forgotten most of the plans we made last time, I said.

That's OK, that's what vacations are for! He replied.

Always aware that things change, I asked: First of all, a couple of questions. Did anything significant change while I was gone? Is the goal still reaching a consensus on software requirements and funding? Are we still on track for getting the right software engineers to attend, and are the draft customer requirements for 2.0 ready to discuss with them?

Yes, it's all a "go," but I'm getting nervous, he said. I saw my boss last night during our two kids' ball game. He asked me if everything was all set for the product development workshop next week. I lied and said that it was! I had to lie to him; no other answer would have been acceptable! But, I am hanging out on this big time, he anxiously concluded.

Don't worry, we'll get it together, I assured, let's get to work.

<u>Adjust and Plan – Clarify Current State and Discuss a Plan</u>
Let's start with the worksheets I developed to guide the technical discussions to the two deliverables, Colin proposed. OK, what are the different deliverables for the two worksheets? I asked. The first worksheet names the four proposed levels of functionality in the left-hand column, and each is followed on a horizontal row that describes the work of coding and testing, what we call a SIPOC (Supplier-Input-Process-Output-Customer series), for each one, he summarized. The next column asks for an estimate of staff hours of effort to develop the 2.0 software functionality described on that row. That estimate will be turned into a budget for each deliverable. Finally, we would accumulate those estimates into a total budget as the first draft amount and then discuss and adjust it in order to put it into next year's budget. What's the second spreadsheet's intended for? I asked. Well, in addition to loading new software on new equipment produced, we need to upgrade hundreds of existing machines in the field. The second worksheet tallies up how many of each old software version there are and their location, he answered. Do you need to consider existing machines in this workshop? They are two different topics, but they both are essential to the deployment, said Colin. Hmm, I stalled waiting for insight, then asked: How might the second worksheet add or detract from discussing the first worksheet? Well, though they are two different but integrated topics, both need to be estimated and added together to make an overall 2.0

deployment plan. OK, so it sounds like the second one is about work that will be implemented later, and the first one is about funding coding of new software for newly manufactured machines. Is that right? I asked. Yeah, that's true. But it's my job to plan for the field upgrades too, And it's a big concern for my boss because he has been getting calls from existing customers who are eager for the update, he said.

Plan and Do – Finalize a Plan and Move into Doing
So the workshop's primary purpose, as I understand it, is to get the software leads to buy into your new model of functionality and fund coding work in next year's budget, right? I asked.

Right, Colin agreed.

So, at this point, is it appropriate to include a worksheet on machines in the field, which will adopt the upgrade in the future? It could lead us down a rabbit trail, and into too great a scope. The software isn't even coded yet, so couldn't planning field downloads come later, like maybe the year after production starts.

True enough. Colin said, It's just that my boss will be pressured by customers for the upgrade and he's already getting anxious about it.

Well, I suggest that we set aside field upgrades for now and focus on the purpose of setting up next year's budget with the leads, and then can worry about the field in another working session. What do you think? I asked.

OK, that makes sense for now, he conceded.

Do and Check Again – Coach During Do, Reflect and Go Again
So, what will be your approach to explain the delay in getting the field software upgrade estimates to your boss? I asked. Colin thought a minute and then said, I'm not sure exactly how I'll handle him. I'll advocate our purpose of getting a budget agreement with the leads and give him our reasoning for a delay in collecting the number of machines in the field. When I meet with him, I'll have to play it as it lays.

Colin's decision to "play it as it lays" with his boss wasn't a cop-out; it was a commitment to stay present despite potential conflict and sell him our planned agenda. In the subsequent meeting his boss reluctantly agreed with our agenda, and in the lean product development workshop, Colin reached a consensus with the software leads to fund new machine functionality in their upcoming annual budgets.

The PDCA or CAP-Do sequence has been integrated into several contemporary coaching models. Three contemporary coaching approaches are the A3, Toyota Kata, and Agile coaching of software coding teams.

Coaching the A3 Problem-Solving Approach

The A3 problem-solving approach consolidates the PDCA model into several steps on a single sheet of paper. A typical A3 is shown in Figure 6.4, but in practice, it is often modified to fit a specific need to consolidate information, plan, and track a project.

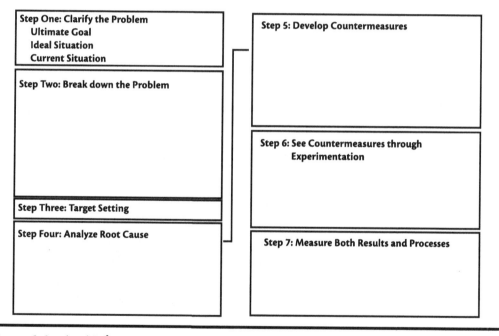

Figure 6.4   An A3 format.

Author John Shook was taught to use the A3 by his Toyota manager in Japan. Here's his description of using it:[9] "The longer I can stay focused on mindfulness of what is happening, the more deeply I can grasp the problem situation. Then, we can get into why, the diagnostic question with a deeper, more accurate and objective inquiry into the situation. When we transition to diagnostic inquiry—asking why something is happening—that's when we start to generate ideas and hypotheses and solicit insights from the team. There's a place for that, but going through the sequence, I think, is something that's very learnable. The A3 form serves as a mechanism for managers to mentor others in root-cause analysis and scientific thinking. The impact of A3 mentoring can also have a meditative effect. The A3 learning process evokes what the Buddhists call beginner's mind."

David Verble, a former Toyota coach, summarizes the challenge of coaching with the A3 this way: "Refrain from assuming that you know more than another human being does about their own work! When you can do this, you shift how you talk with people, ask so many more questions, and help everyone (yourself included) learn. Simple, right? Sure. But again, doing this consistently is hard work."[10] A manager or lean coach might encourage an individual or team to start an A3 in order to jump-start collaboration across multiple functions or locations. Here's the testimony of a product development coach who considered his company's use of the A3 to be a core strength of its product development system.

> The A3 methodology is a problem-solving and people-engagement process. One way it is helping our product leaders is that the A3 process defines the paths through a design process for new, complex products or business changes. Leaders get together to kick off each A3 as a logical thought process, which aligns everyone involved on a project's purpose, problem statement, and deliverables. What you're doing with this series of A3s is collaborating with people and using either an engagement A3 or a problem-solving A3 to plan and track progress. Both A3 types can be used virtually online, yet personal relationships among a team are key to developing them to be successful. We use them to identify and relieve constraints, and help us surface and mitigate risks. For example, after a strategy for a new product program is defined, we develop a portfolio of A3s that identify the gaps or unknowns we face so that we understand the risks. The A3s clarify the essential elements for executing a program's key enablers, and then people work them. We review status A3s to communicate the current state of each member's work in conference calls, and then each one posts them online. Any member can go online at any time and review an A3 that is being developed thousands of miles away. Periodic face-to-face meetings with all involved help sustain each individual's commitment to a common goal and maintain an esprit

de corps. When people work in different locations, they'll remember the evening they were together, went out to dinner, and told stories about each other's families. These working relationships stay with them as they work their A3s and communicate them over time. For us, A3s are essential drivers of success.

Here's the same coach's reflection on his company's utilization of the A3 in product development some four years later.

What I said several years ago still applies, but only in a few pockets, and overall I believe we have digressed a bit. In reflecting on this I think several potential root causes are in play. One of the big challenges is the typical engineer's ego. Engineers fancy themselves to be great problem solvers, but they tend to quickly jump to solutions. Many times you'll see them move from the problem statement on an A3 to solutions and forego the analysis & root cause determination. Some see the A3 document's steps as non-value added work, rather than a systematic method. Besides, it's easier to slap together slides and present a quick solution proposal, rather than do a rigorous A3. Unless their leaders are well versed in problem solving, the lack of good root cause investigation will go unnoticed. In reflecting on this, I wonder if we did an adequate job of coaching and mentoring so that everyone, especially managers, experienced the value of the methodology?

The Improvement Kata and the Coaching Kata

A "kata" is a Japanese word for "good form," and each one offers a standard procedure for learning an aspect of a specific skill set. It's a term well known in the martial arts and it's practiced (without the term) in the field of elite sports training. For example, a baseball coach might aim to develop a pitcher's skill for keeping his pitches low, where they are more difficult for a batter to hit. He would observe a pitcher's wind up, release point, and follow through and then would introduce a new routine to practice, often called a "drill." Later the coach would return to check progress and eventually offer another drill (similar to the next kata).

In his book *Toyota Kata*,[11] author Mike Rother described the unseen managerial coaching routine behind Toyota's success."[12] He distilled their standard continuous improvement coaching down to a series of basic questions: (1) What is the target condition? (2) What is the actual condition now? (3) What obstacles do you think are preventing you from reaching the target condition? (4) What is your next step or next experiment? (5) What do you expect and how quickly can we go and see what we have learned from taking that next step? In kata, the coach sets a goal and encourages a "check" before iterating scientific thinking. In a dialogue, a coach uses the five questions, plus clarifying follow-up conversation, to help a job performer or team improve a process. Kata coach David Rau described his evolution from being a technical expert to becoming a kata coach:[13]

> In my early days as a coach I based my approach on the expert model, what we now call "coaching for correction." As an expert in manufacturing, I'd help a worker by analyzing a needed repair, order materials, do the repair, and be a hero. However, weeks or months later, when I worked my way back to the unit where I'd provided an expert solution, it had degraded. Why? Number one, sometimes I didn't get the right outcome because I didn't fully understand the root cause of the problem. Number two, nobody else had learned the underlying paradigm of problem solving, so later, they couldn't continue to improve upon the initial solution. Nevertheless, in the expert way of coaching, sometimes I'd find a big problem, a "train wreck" in the process, so to speak, and I would guide employees to review and correct the situation, putting every single rail car back on the track. I would often start by observing how employees went about solving problems in producing our technical manuals, and then I would explain to them what I would have done. This approach mostly succeeded with people who were just like me. However, a better way was to enable them to find the fault for a quality breakdown in the process themselves. Then, they would learn scientific thinking.
>
> The coaching kata is a way to help employees break down a process or quality problem with many unknowns so that they can improve a process's performance step by step. In producing a trouble-shooting manual, for example, the operations manager or coach first defines the challenge to be met. Often it's a gap to be closed, and this gives the kata work a direction. For example, if the goal is to reduce the number of first-pass quality-control markups by 50 percent, I need to understand which type of quality problem is the most significant in the service manual involved.

If I, as a coach, looked at the quality issues, and say that they were all of equal priority, I might stratify the sections of our service manual to learn which part of it is most often the source of errors. Then during a first kata coaching event, I might focus an individual or a team on learning the root cause of that section's errors. Then, I would ask: Do we have enough information to set a target condition for quality in the "researching and authoring" stage of that particular section? If we did, a target condition would be drafted, such as reducing errors in that section by 75 percent. Here's a table I made to guide my thinking and the clarifying questions I sometimes use during kata coaching.

	Kata Coach's Thinking	*Kata Coach's Questions*
Vision	What an organization need is being met?	What is this particular challenge?
Challenge	Does the target condition fit the challenge?	What is the target condition, and why?
Obstacle	Is there a reason for the obstacle selected?	Which obstacle are we working on?
Experiment	Is the proposed experiment capable of generating learning relevant to the obstacle?	How are you thinking about the experiment now?
Go and See	What's really happening?	When can we go and see what you have learned?
Correction	Is it best for this learner at this time to be corrected, or will he or she benefit from failing?	Where do you go from here?

When we first started moving toward a lean operation, we had a low-trust culture. Despite everyone putting on a happy face, there was a pervasive, dark attitude behind their masks and for many trust was zero. To have a chance at teaching leaders to coach, I first had to work with employees on what was important to them. In the first two years, I worked to build trust and strengthen their scientific thinking and problem-solving skills. My job was to help them sustain a chain of integrity in problem solving.

At first, for instance, a project manager would often come to me with an idea for a solution. When they did, I'd say: That's good but treat it as a hypothesis and try to disprove it. Later, I began asking them the five kata questions so that they would focus on identifying and prioritizing the biggest obstacles to document quality in a technical manual.

Lean is a two-pronged approach: respect people and improve the work process. Early on I had to spend years getting our managers out of the old command-and-control approach. It's a fear-based means of making money. The lean process requires managers to have the value of "respect for humanity," which includes employees, customers, and me personally, because I want to be respected too. I want to lead change in a way that we all gain from improvements. Just aiming for lean coaching to add shareholder value is a crock.

Leadership's Role in Kata Coaching

Kata coaching has proven able to move a local operation into steady value-added work. Its scope is set by a site leadership team who has a strategic direction, an operational vision, and a set of high-priority challenges for key value streams or work centers. Figure 6.5 illustrates how

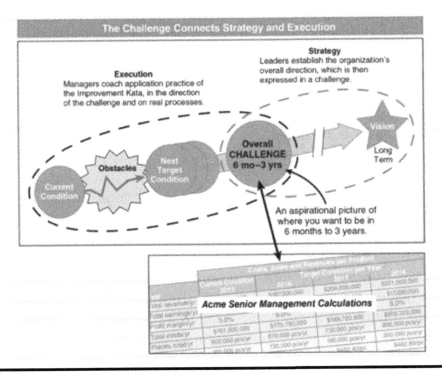

Figure 6.5   Linking strategy to execution to kata. © Copyright at *Toyota Kata Culture,* Mike Rother and Gerd Aulinger, McGraw Hill Education, 2017, p. 21. Used with permission.

an organization's strategy moves between the poles of a long-term vision and a set of overall challenges with a time frame of six months and three years.[14]

In starting kata coaching in an enterprise, a leadership team sets up an "advance group," a set of people who first learn and practice the improvement kata on actual work processes. When they have enough experience, they investigate the question: "What are we learning about the applying the improvement kata in our processes, with our people, and in our organization?"[15] Their purpose is to identify and eliminate obstacles to embedding kata coaching in their operation. The advance group's planning might last between two and six months.[16] Kata coaching consultant Beth Carrington uses the graphic in Figure 6.6 to orient leadership teams and advance groups about connecting a vision to the threshold of knowledge and daily PDCA.

A focus on continuous improvement proceeds down from a long-term vision to daily improvement following PDCA:[17] (1) Create a long-term vision that sets the direction for process and systems improvement; (2) focus the process on one or two mid-term challenges (six months to three years) that a targeted operation, value stream, value stream loop, department, or product area needs to achieve; (3) identify all the related value streams or

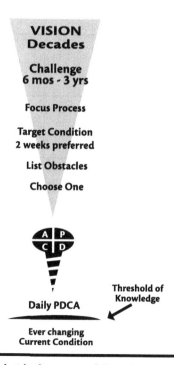

Figure 6.6 Getting to the point in kata coaching. © Copyright Beth Carrington. Used with permission.

processes that are in the scope of the challenge; (4) select the managers and employees to participate in the initial kata cadre; (5) train and mentor this group until it has enough coaching experience to become proficient; (6) select a few of this initial group to be the first kata coaches; and (7) this initial group uses the coaching kata to help teams learn to find improvements at the threshold of knowledge.

During continuous improvement, an experienced coach may serve as a "second coach," that is, be a mentor for a new kata coach. A second coach will often ask herself questions including: What's the situation with the process or the learner now?" "How is the coach thinking?" And, "What does the individual need to learn?"[18]

Business unit or value stream managers facilitate a daily progress discussion with their coaches using a summary board in an office or dedicated conference room wall. The coaches post summary cards on it as illustrated in Figure 6.7.[19] In a brief daily meeting, coaches review their updated cards and receive coaching from their manager or a second coach.

Level	Learner	Coach	Target Condition & Date	Current				Next	
				Day/Week	Day/Week	Day/Week	Day/Week	Day/Week	Day/Week
Value Stream	Coaching Summary Card	Coaching Summary Card							**Target**
V/S Loop	Coaching Summary Card								
Process	Coaching Summary Card								

Figure 6.7   Coaching summary board. © Copyright at *Toyota Kata Culture*, **Mike Rother and Gerd Aulinger, McGraw Hill Education, 2017, p. 99. Used with permission.**

Kata coaching in an organization is fractal; that is, it should be practiced from the shop floor teams up through the executive level – who should rethink corporate business processes and support systems. However, not all executives practice the kata they preach. Ms. Carrington cites the time when it dawned on her that sponsoring executives didn't apply the kata and scientific thinking to improve their own higher-level work processes:[20] "I did a follow-up visit at one global organization that had been practicing kata for two years. They were doing the practice at lower levels with coaching and second coaching. My big "ah ha" moment was when I recognized that managers were using MBO at their own level and kata coaching down 2 or 3 levels. It was practicing scientific thinking/experimenting at the process level but implementation mode at the leadership level. Kata practice wasn't seen as something they needed to do. In my thinking, they didn't get kata's cultural piece, as something for everyone to practice."

In kata, everyone at every level needs to coach others within their own purview, find their current threshold of knowledge, apply the five questions, and employ their kaizen minds in order to improve both the process and the work system.

Coaching Agile Teams

The Agile Manifesto[21] was drafted around the turn of the century by thought leaders as they were enjoying time at a ski resort. In their agile approach to software development, work isn't expected to progress smoothly, but is analogous to skiing over packed moguls on a fast downhill run. Agile acknowledges that bumps of uncertainty will exist during development due to evolving customer needs, internal company challenges or constraints, plus new learning, and as a result, priorities should frequently change. Building on the combined learning of numerous experimenters, including Jeff Sutherland and others, Ken Schwaber and Mike Beedle described agile coaching in *Agile Software Development with Scrum* in 2001.[22] They advocate that software development should be a flexible flow of work "sprints" in a brief time window. During a sprint, a development team works and captures new learning in daily stand-up meetings.

Mary and Tom Poppendieck, coauthors of *Lean Software Development: An Agile Toolkit*,[23] described several lean principles in the Agile method: (1) Business people and developers collaborate daily; (2) agile creates sustainable, predictable development timelines, helping the team maintain a constant pace; (3) motivated individuals build projects as a team, which is given the support it needs; (4) teams convey information in face-to-face conversation; and (5) at regular intervals, the team reflects and adjusts its behavior accordingly.

The table below summarizes the learning and insights gained by a software product manager and his agile coach during their experience starting

Software Product Manager	Agile Coach
Planning	
We want to be predictive; that is, we want to deliver quality software when we say we will. We divide the work into deliverable objectives for functionality and assign coders to meet them during our quarterly program planning meetings. Both customers and Agile teams want to get more functions in our software. However, sooner or later, you've got to tune out the engineers, decide the minimum amount of value the customer can accept, and get on with it. It takes a lot of work to get from a high-level description to something a person can code. Agile is purposeful and practical and keeps software development simple – if managers will keep it that way.	Predictability can be a challenge for coding teams. In a matrix organization, component teams often have difficulty getting all the coded pieces to come together in a designed value stream. It is only when all the pieces come together that we can understand how well a feature works. In order to confront this challenge, we must align each individual and team workflow to pull the requested value through the organization. The idea is that we prioritize the customer-facing value that we want to deliver in a short time. Then, we bring all the affected component teams together to align on the technical details necessary to provide this value and decide how to best execute solutions in an appropriate time frame.
Doing	
We make sure we get the most important stuff done first. Most of the time, this approach allows us to get the hard stuff done, and none of the other stuff matters if we don't get that. So, we first get a minimum feature-set that is good enough to ship. We keep building on it until we get something that is commercially viable. Effective leaders strive to understand the world from their team's perspective – the challenges from their point of view.	You're trying to get an inside-out view of the work, so you can bridge it to your outside-in view and identify gaps. Then, we must find ways to reflect these gaps to the team in such a way that they want to confront them. Once teams understand the gaps and the pain that those gaps are causing, they want to address the pain with change.

(Continued)

Software Product Manager		Agile Coach
Checking		
I talk to the key players every day, those who are leading the systems integration, the software coding, and the testing. There is a lot of noise that I have to filter out. When I speak to them, I ask, "Did we do what we said we were going to do this week?" Not helping customers is unacceptable, and in Agile, we can't delay. We cut out features at times and leave a few small problems for short durations. For me, Agile kind of comes down to: Can we adjust and do what we say we are going to do?		When teams are working well together, it is easy for them to feel that everything is optimized. Knowledge work is difficult to schedule and requires management to check and maintain synchronization between Agile teams and to limit team conflict. We use daily stand-up meetings to review an issues list and check on follow-up for multiple component teams. Discoveries and setbacks are inevitable in the development process because of the innovative nature of the work. Effective coaching enables more self-management within the targeted software iteration.
Adjusting		
My big aha was that, rather than pushing for management's goals, I ask, "What does the team need now to deliver the required technical solutions?" Giving or finding that support becomes my purpose. Once we get more familiar and knowledgeable about Agile, we'll probably adjust and do bigger chunks of software. However, for now, smaller chunks are all we are competent to handle.		Retrospectives are a powerful tool to make adjustments in this space. For our first quarterly meeting, we hung a large wall chart, three butcher papers high, and placed post-it notes to identify the work that needed to be done. In doing that, we found a huge number of problems and misalignments. At times, the conversations were challenging, but facing this pain, we created unity and alignment across teams. They created a catalyst for change, and now the team is saying that they want to make them even better.

a new Agile team. Their observations are sequenced in the PDCA format for planning, doing, checking, and adjusting.

In the case above, the product manager learned to honestly assess coding status and issues, update executives, and renegotiate timing and deliverables with customers when necessary. He shifted his purpose from pleasing his boss to supporting the team. The Agile coach summarized the new team's progress this way: "We have gone through months of development, and this team is kicking some butt. We have come a long way."

The Deliberate Practice of Purpose

Quality guru W. Edwards Deming's first principle was: "Create constancy of purpose toward improvement of product and service." So the second deliberate practice of lean coaching is having a purpose, that is, a process or quality target that can be measured by a metric. Before beginning a coaching session, a lean coach might consider a few questions to focus and find a purpose such as: (1) What is our long-term vision, and what are the related near-term challenges? (2) What are the short-term deliverables or milestones in existing plans? (3) What is the next problem to solve? (4) What deliverables do the sponsors and executives want? (5) What do customers need?

As coaches engage job performers and teams in continuous improvement, disruptive people and distractions can divert their focus onto other goals, "shiny objects", "nice to do" things that are not needed or timely. So, coaches must stay mindful of their purpose even as things change during a coaching engagement. Author Kiyo Suzaki suggests that a simple "so what" line of inquiry can drill down and clarify a coaching purpose.[24]

Question: Why am I doing this task?
Answer: Because my boss asked me to do it.

So what?
If I complete the task and do it well, I will make progress on an important project.

So what?
The project is essential to a critical customer who is vital to our business.

So what?
I find meaning and purpose in our mission to deliver value to our customers, so I'm going to do this work task to the best of my ability.

When a "so what" question evokes an "I don't know" answer, a coach should review facts and data, go to see the actual situation, meet with knowledgeable people, and clarify a purpose. In the value stream mapping case below, I stayed mindful and was able to shift the lean event's purpose and agenda on the fly.

> On the first morning of the quality function's lean event, I had the quality staff draw a process map of their recent engagement with a product engineering design group. As usual, they noted the process flow along with the waste and posted problems in their engagement with product design teams. However, I became mindful that something wasn't going well. The group seemed reluctant to speak up while their manager was in the room, so I asked him to leave for a while, which he willingly agreed to do. Then, I asked the team: Why is there so little interest in this?
>
> After a long pause, Ty, the informal leader of the group, finally said: In negotiating with the company's various product executives our manager won't specify that their product engineers must dedicate time to quality workshops. As a result, the product engineers often refuse to commit time to identify product failure modes and we have to interview them catch-as-catch-can, often at their desks amidst phone calls and such. Why is this going on? I asked. Ty hesitated but then disclosed:
>
> Our boss has a single overriding goal – to get our staff assigned to billable engineering projects to help his budget. When the product engineers see that their divisional boss is minimally committed to the quality analysis, they view it as a "check the box" exercise.
>
> Based on this new problem to solve, I shelved the process improvement and asked the staff to draft a new purpose statement for their quality function and a set of guiding principles for future contracting with the company's engineering divisions. Later, when their manager returned to the meeting, he agreed with the team's new purpose statement and contracting principles.

In my haste, I had assumed that the quality team needed process improvement (Doesn't everyone?), but their problem lay elsewhere! It took until the middle of the first day, as I listened to the team and watched their body language, for me to see that something was wrong. In fact, their main problem wasn't a process issue, it was bureaucracy and the politics of contracting and getting paid in internal budget funds. The QA manager was so focused on cutting deals to offset his staff's salary that he wasn't clear with product executives that they were required to make time for their engineers to do a FMEA quality analyses (failure-mode effects analysis) with his staff. Note that I could have avoided the lost time in the event and improvising the agenda had I done a better setup of the event.

The Deliberate Practice of Mindfulness

The third deliberate practice of lean coaching is mindfulness. Author Sharon Salzberg defines it this way:[25]

> Mindfulness is that place in the middle, where we are neither consumed by nor reject what is going on. We have the ability to be fully present such that we're interested in what's going on, but we're not forming judgments or dashing off into proliferation of thoughts. By being with what is, we can create a space where creativity arises, where other options arise.

Mindfulness at work is the skill of setting aside one's own agenda, expectations, and role and simply observing "what is" in the behavior of a person, events, formal communications or on-going tasks during a work activity. The value of mindfulness is that it enables a coach to track progress and setbacks in an ongoing coaching engagement in order to adapt a purpose or ask better questions along the way.

Lean coach Mike Orzen recommends that a coach use the following four steps to establish mindfulness:[26] (1) Begin calming your mind by taking a few slow breaths. Don't try to change your breathing by making it deeper, just slow it down; (2) focus on an object and attempt to remain focused on just that object for as long as possible. It's OK to blink (and keep breathing); (3) notice when your mind starts to wander and begins to think about things other than the object. It is normal and natural for the mind to wander; (4) as you notice your mental focus has drifted, simply bring it back to the object.

In another case, I was coaching a workshop, one which I believed was going along swimmingly. However, when I stepped back and became mindful I realized that I didn't really understand the problem that we were trying to solve, nor did anyone else. Here's the story.

I was in a meeting with a CEO and his leadership team, working to develop a skills map for machinists' training at an aerospace company. We had planned to identify the skill-area topics within machining work and then define three levels of competency for each. However, almost immediately the leadership team began solving problems fast and furious. I sensed that they were on the wrong track. While others at the table were talking, I slowed down, took a few deep breaths, became mindful, let go of self-concern that I might look bad, and saw my mistake. An insight told me that the discussion was rushing to some solution, even though we didn't know the root cause. Neither I nor the members of the leadership team had ask why the machinists didn't seem motivated enough to learn the new skills the company needed for the future. I halted the table discussion, saying: Let's do a 5-Why exercise to understand why machinists aren't seeking to learn higher-level skills already?

Answering the first "why" the team leads claimed that the underlying cause was employees' lack of motivation. Why do they lack motivation? I asked. In the discussion that followed we discovered several possible reasons. Previously, when they became discouraged with new employees' initial clumsy attempts to program a CNC machine the leads wrote them off as "unteachable." Second, the company had published only very general descriptions of the machining skills, they weren't specific enough to enable workers to focus, study and learn on their own. Third, the leads had their own work to do, so when a machinist became confused or took too long to learn, they went to another machine to catch up on it.

Once the leadership team discussed these underlying causes, they outlined counter-measures for all three. First, the team leads agreed to be more patient when coaching the hands-on curriculum. Second, management commit-ted to defining a specific menu of machining topics and skills, within three escalating bands of capability. They set a target date for a plant-wide orientation for machinists in which a detailed curriculum would be announced and the team leads would pledge to be more patient. Third, the CEO committed to making more of the team leaders' time available to teach during the work week. The leadership group met with the machinists to share the plan and get feedback at the end of the following month and the team leads soon began a new round of hands-on training targeted on the clarified skill bands.

Why Is It So Difficult to Stay Mindful?

Why is it so difficult to stay mindful? A Google search recently estimated that our human minds normally experience about 60,000 thoughts, impressions, and feelings every day, and without training, they crowd out mindfulness out. Recently, researcher Jordan Poppenk measured the duration of his research subjects' actual thoughts by defining a boundary for each. He found an average of 6200 thoughts per day on average – one about every 10 waking seconds or so. (https://www.newsweek.com/humans-6000-thoughts-every-day-1517963). Another reason we can't stay mindful was found over two centuries ago, when renaissance philosopher David Hume wrote that we humans are run by our passions, not our reason. Contemporary author Robert Wright details how it works: "Our reasoning faculty isn't really in charge; its agenda – what it reasons about – is set by feelings, and it can influence our behavior only by influencing our feelings."[27]

So our emotions trigger excessive thinking, which, in turn, swings back and causes even more feelings, and both obstruct mindfulness. As sketched in Figure 6.8, they are like a teeter-totter in the brain. However, feelings aren't bad; in fact, they are a form of human intelligence. Feelings aren't necessarily "right", rather, they're a "quick take" on reality, one that can provide a vital information on how to respond to a situation or survive a threat. While valid as signals to pay attention, feelings can be biased and thus need to be tested with reason or experiments to establish their validity and worth. Lowering down the other side of the teeter-totter, if we lack feelings to weigh or prioritize our thoughts, unfocused thinking can lead to mistakes or a fall into paralysis by analysis.

Figure 6.8   A teeter-totter in the brain.

When we swing back and forth between negative feelings and excess thinking, we are caught in what is commonly called a "story." Say your boss criticizes you for missing a project milestone, and yet it wasn't your fault. Perhaps he had required you to hire a supplier who subsequently became late. The result might be a resentful story about how unjust his criticism was and rising worry about your job security.

Author Melanie Greenberg writes that worry is the cognitive component of anxiety.[28] It's defined as: "A feeling of worry, nervousness, or unease, typically about an imminent event or something with an uncertain outcome."[29] A Gallup poll found that 45 percent of Americans surveyed reported that they had felt "a lot" of worry during the workday.[30] My worry arises, for example, when my boss texts saying, "I need to see you in my office right away!" However, worry isn't all bad; it can motivate needed action, for example, when it makes me plan my taxes early.

Worry causes stress, which author David Gelles defines as: "A stress response is an automatic, reptilian, lizard-brain, dinosaur response to some stressful thing."[31] A survey by the American Psychological Association found that 69 percent of employees view their work as a significant source of stress, and more than half said that it reduced their productivity.[32] For example, a manager planning an important presentation may feel rising stress peak just before it happens. A supply-base manager might feel the anxiety that triggers stress when a supplier delivery is late. An information tech manager might experience pressure when bug fixes have depleted her budget, and there is no money left to purchase the software upgrades she promised to users. A project manager might feel stress when he realizes that he is going to miss a project milestone, one that's the subject of an upcoming review.

Researchers Shira Bar and Moshe Bar had subjects free-associate words while holding extra thoughts in memory, what they called a "high-load" mental condition.[33] They summarized that: "The capacity for original and creative thinking is markedly stymied by stray thoughts, obsessive ruminations, and other forms of mental load." Similarly, a study by neuroscientists at the University of Pittsburgh found that anxiety and stress hurt performance because they disengage the prefrontal cortex, which is the decision-making and problem-solving aspects of the brain.[34] And a stressed-out mind imagines problems that don't even exist, adding to a vicious downward cycle into stress. Psychologist Kelly McGonigal contends that the best way to handle it is to face it directly in the near term. She writes: "The best way to manage stress isn't to reduce or avoid it, but rather to rethink and even embrace it."[35] Stress impacts a person's performance in an inverted "U" shape. At first, more stress leads to more effort and higher performance (which is why the blame game works for a brief time). When stress becomes too much for an individual to tolerate, his or her performance sinks to the bottom of the "U." But when an individual can strengthen and tolerate stressful situations or even embrace them as a "challenge," he or she moves up the right side of the "U" curve and into high performance.

I'll use the children's game of rock-paper-scissors, shown in Figure 6.9, as a metaphor to understand how mindfulness cuts the negative feelings and excess thought that creates worry and stress. In Western culture, we are taught in school that thinking should be rock-solid, so let's allow thinking be the "rock" on the left side of the model. Moving around the bottom of the circle, when thinking becomes excessive, its density crushes our mindfulness, destroying the "scissors," so "rock crushes scissors." When mindfulness has been crushed in this way, "scissors" aren't available to cut the "paper," that is, cut off negative feelings as they arise. Then, negative feelings swing over the top of the circle and paper covers rock, that is, thinking becomes irrational or lost in emotional stories.[36]

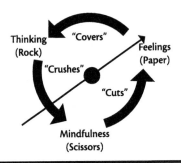

Figure 6.9   Rock-paper-scissors in the brain.

However, when a leader can make mindfulness her default mental state, shown at the bottom of the circle, it cuts away the psychological debris of excess thoughts and negative feelings, thus eliminating the stories that cause anxiety, worry and stress.

Here is a case from a time when mindfulness reduced my worry about working with a challenging partner and led to success.

> Dave and I were never close. He was a lean coach and a six-sigma black belt, one highly dedicated to working with facts and data. When we were assigned by our mutual boss to plan a strategy meeting for an aftermarket parts division in an automotive corporation, I felt that working with him was going to be a challenge

for me. However, I resolved to set aside my judgment and stay mindful, and as I listened to his ideas, and fairly considered them, lo and behold he was often right! I discovered that he asked excellent questions, ones that made me think harder and better about the upcoming strategy session. By showing him respect and staying mindful, we became complimentary partners, and later the strategic planning event was a success.

What's the take-away? When a coach makes mindfulness her default state of mind, she can notice arising thoughts and feelings, apply reason, and shift the purpose or process of coaching in real time.

Can Lean Coaches Start and Sustain Lean Startups?

During the last decade or so, Western enterprise executives and plant managers have hired lean coaches and given them a mandate to implement lean thinking in their business operations. However, the question is: "Can lean coaches start and sustain lean work processes and systems on their own?"

Sitting around tables at lean conferences in recent years, I've had lots of discussions with lean coaches. Away from work, many express their frustrations with their bosses, even the ones that hired them. Many of their managers understand lean operations as a way to reduce costs and increase quality but lack a grasp of the philosophy and complimentary coaching approach that sustain lean work. Clinging to command and control or its philosophical offspring, the pragmatic-empirical management style, they fail to create social conditions compatible with learning. Here's the voice of an American coach who struggled to start or sustain lean operations in a succession of companies.[37]

> I would love to have a lean success story to tell, but all my attempts at lean transformation have failed. My first try at implementing lean production was in a company startup. The company made an implantable medical device, which consisted of an electronic circuit board that was encased in a mold, machined to the right size, and then covered with a bio-interface. I created the process map, calculated the amount of material needed by each successive step, and then adjusted the process's pace to meet anticipated customer sales. Management was on board with the new

production process, and we were ready to quickly scale up to full production. Unfortunately, the product didn't pass the clinical trials, and we never ran and tested the plan.

A second lean startup experience couldn't have been more different. The operations manager claimed he wanted a complete value stream map that showed a balanced line. However, the president wanted to push the product through a few clinical trials and sell it quickly so that he could get a bonus payout. After creating a value stream map that covered four walls of a small conference room, the lean project was sacked.

My third lean coaching job was at an older company that was stuck in its ways. They were still doing work the old-fashioned way, and they had no intention of changing. Managers had no idea how long any process took to go through production, and they built all the parts needed to meet shipment demands in big batches. We mapped the travel through the process and found that the product moved two miles up, down, and across the manufacturing floor. On this job, I engaged senior management and started by training all the operators. The project appeared to be going well, but the most significant gap remained among the functional managers who had not bought into the lean approach. As soon as a lean line had a few issues and failed to produce planned results, they turned against it. The failure had nothing to do with lean; it was due to politics and bureaucratic budgets.

Finally, as a new lean coach in another biomedical company, I joined an operation that claimed to have lean production in place. The problem was that managers were so bottom-line oriented that even though they had the training, did kaizen events and held daily shift startup meetings, they didn't fully understand lean production. They were focused on cost savings. In trying to bring lean into U.S. companies, I've been up against the short-term thinking of management in various flavors every time.

Reflection: What Can We Learn from Lean Coaching?

Lean coaching has proven effective in iterating continuous improvement in work processes. However, often executives and site leadership team members harbor conflicting visions and various leadership philosophies and their conflict stalls or stops middle managers or specialists from providing support, or prevents the linking of an extended value stream. As a result, lean successes are often limited in scope and don't spread to full value streams or across operating facilities in a corporation. So, the next problem to solve is finding a way to get all executives and managers on the same page. The fourth key to implementing a lean operational transformation in a Western business is change leadership.

What You Can Do

If your enterprise sponsors a standard coaching approach, learn it, practice it, and periodically meet with a manager or second coach to review your progress. Encourage enterprise executives to identify leadership behaviors and management systems that will be obstacles to successful lean work startups, and counter them early. Encourage higher managers to use a coaching approach to improve enterprise policies and systems so that they support a lean operation.

Notes

1 *Lean Thinking*, James Womack and Daniel Jones, Simon and Shuster, 1996, p. 10.
2 Cited in *The Way of Zen*, Alan Watts, Vintage Books Edition, 1989, Pantheon Books, 1957, p. 17.
3 *See Leading the Lean Enterprise Transformation*, George Koenigsaecker, CRC Press, A Productivity Press Book, Taylor & Francis, 2013, Appendix G, pp. 221–234.
4 Mike Ward phone interview in 2014.
5 Presentation at the AME conference, San Diego, CA, 2018.
6 Jim Bickerstaff interview at Autoliv Americas in Ogden, UT, 2017.
7 Gung Ho (released in Australia as Working Class Man) is a 1986 American comedy film directed by Ron Howard and starring Michael Keaton.
8 *Autoliv, Empowered to Solve Problems, Kathy Whitehead and Scott Saxton, in Leading the Lean Enterprise Transformation*, George Koenigsaecker, CRC Press, Taylor & Francis Group, A Productivity Press Book, 2013, pp. 221–234.
9 *Thoughts on Coaching from John Shook and Edgar Schein*, LEI Post, Lean Leaper, July 2, 2018.
10 *Coaching Is Work*, David Verble, Published on February 6, 2020, Linked-in.
11 *Toyota Kata*, Mike Rother, McGraw-Hill, 2010, p. 246.

12 *The Improvement Model*, Mike Rother, Toyota Kata.com, July 2014.

13 David Rau interview in 2016.

14 *Thanks to Mike Rother for Sharing This Diagram from Toyota Kata Culture*, Mike Rother and Gerd Aulinger, McGraw-Hill Education, 2017, p. 21.

15 *Toyota Kata*, Mike Rother, McGraw-Hill, 2010, p. 245.

16 *Toyota Kata*, Mike Rother, McGraw-Hill, 2010, p. 246.

17 Phone interview in March 2020.

18 *Toyota Kata*, Mike Rother, McGraw-Hill, 2010, p. 192.

19 *Toyota Kata Culture*, Mike Rother and Gerd Aulinger, McGraw-Hill Education, 2017, p. 121.

20 Phone interview in March 2020.

21 Agile Manifesto outlines 4 values and 12 principles for teams, Google.

22 *Agile Software Development with Scrum*, Ken Schwaber and Mike Beedle, Prentice Hall PTR, 2001.

23 *Lean Software Development: An Agile Toolkit*, Mary Poppendieck and Tom Poppendieck Addison Wesley, 2003.

24 *Results from the Heart*, Kiyoshi Suzaki, The Free Press, 2002, p. 7, 9.

25 *Defining Mindfulness*, Sharon Salzberg, Tricycle Magazine, March 10, 2020.

26 Doing Versus Being – How Mindfulness Supports Better Lean Thinking, Part 2, Mike Orzen, LEI.org.

27 *Why Buddhism Is True*, Robert Wright, Simon and Shuster, 2017, p. 130.

28 *The Five Secrets to a Stress-Proof Brain*, Psychology Today, xxx, February 05, 2017.

29 Google; Dictionary.

30 *Americans Are Among the Most Stressed People in the World*, Poll Finds, Niraj Chokshi, New York Times, April 25, 2019.

31 *Mindful Work*, David Gelles, An Eamon Dolan Book, Houghton Miffilin Harcourt, 2015, p. 83.

32 Cited in *Mindful Work*, David Gelles, An Eamon Dolan Book, Houghton Miffilin Harcourt, 2015, p. 82.

33 *Think Less, Think Better, Moshe Bar*, New York Times, June 17, 2016 cited in Associate Activation and Its Relation to Exploration and Exploitation of the Brain, Shira Bar and Moshe Bar, *Psychological Science*, June 2016, Vol. 27, No. 6, pp. 776–789.

34 *Just Made a Bad Decision?* Joe Miksch, University of Pittsburgh News Services.

35 *The Upside of Stress: Why Stress Is Good for You, and How to Get. Good at It*, Kelly McGonigal, Avery, an imprint of Penguin Random House, 2015, p. xxi.

36 The dot in the center of the model represents the present moment and the arrow signifies one being present in the flow.

37 Anonymous.

Chapter 7

The Fourth Key Is Change Leadership

When you are present, when your attention is fully in the now, that presence will flow into you and transform what you do. There will be quality and power in it.[1]

Eckhart Tolle

Flow provides a rare chance to take an active involvement in something larger than the self, without relinquishing any of one's mental, physical, or volitional skills.[2]

Mihaly Csikszentmihalyi

Compassion reduces our fear, boosts our confidence, and brings us inner strength. By reducing distrust, it opens us to others and brings us a sense of connection with them and a sense of purpose and meaning in life.[3]

Dalai Lama

IN THE TENNESSEE PLANT

When I arrived to facilitate the kaizen event on line four, a dozen union members had already arrived in the upstairs conference room, but at 7:30, there was only one supervisor was in a seat.

It wasn't even 7:31 when a union guy in the front asked: Where are the rest of the supervisors?

Having been away during the planning the week before, I just said: I have no idea.

What are you going to do about it? he challenged. He had a point. Under pressure, I said: OK, if I can't get more supervisors to attend, I'll reschedule the event.

On my way out the door I spoke with flat affect: I'll be back in a few minutes.

I took the stairs down to the shop floor and started walking toward the front of the building. As I made my way to the plant manager's corner office, I knew that the upcoming discussion could easily be my last act on the job. As I approached his administrative assistant, she gave me a friendly smile and said: Go on in. If she had been aware of my intention, she might have blocked the door.

After a quick hello to Chuck (the initial plant manager), I just said: The line-four kaizen event upstairs has twelve union workers and only one supervisor. It's not good enough.

There was a long pause. He said nothing, but he held eye contact with me for a few tense seconds. He communicated his displeasure with a stern face.

Then he picked up the phone and muttered: I'll take care of it.

Fifteen minutes later, I had a full complement of 12 managers in the upstairs conference room. Afterward, they all agreed that the two days were a success, yet that wasn't the end of the story.

During the following week, a union man taunted Chuck, saying that I had threatened to cancel the workshop. He didn't believe it, so he called me at home and ask:

Did you threaten to cancel the kaizen on line four last week? They said you did.

Staying present in the face of conflict, I said: Yeah, I told them that if we couldn't get an equal number of managers and union members that I would reschedule it.

Without pause he then said: Well I won't be needing your services anymore.

I immediately accepted his decision and saw the next challenge on the horizon so I asked him: What will you say to my consulting boss about this?

Well, I am not happy about it, he said, but at least you were honest.

I was disappointed to lose the work of course, but I felt I had no choice but to be honest. Funny, despite being fired, I didn't feel bad. I had done my best and led out of my values. I had paid a price, but that cost turned out to be a good investment. A month later, Chuck was transferred and demoted, and when the new plant manager arrived in Tennessee, the union president asked that I be reinstated as the plant's lean consultant. Yet a third chapter of the story was still to come.

Not long afterward, I was asked to take on lead responsibility for consulting at the very plant where Chuck had been transferred. On the morning I arrived there, I immediately moved to face the looming conflict. As I walked down the hall toward his office, I let go of self-concern and entered a state of presence. I had no goal other than being aware and responding appropriately to any lingering anger he might feel.

When I arrived at his open office door, Chuck didn't seem surprised to see me. He had heard that I was coming, and he invited me to take a seat. After we chatted a long while about his new job, he asked me to join him and his wife for dinner at his new condo overlooking Lake Michigan that evening. I got the sense that because we had both spoken honestly during our conflict in Tennessee, we shared a mutual respect.

The story illustrates how two leaders who can stay present and face conflict will come out with a better relationship (a fact confirmed by social science research). However, when executives or members of a site leadership team avoid conflict due to different operational visions or leadership philosophies, a discordant message will be pushed down to their respective middle managers and support staff. Then, rather than providing quick support for coaches and new lean startups, they continue to prioritize project work in their "silo." As a result, when new lean processes stall or stop, they will be discredited in the eyes of many. So in order for lean startups to be sustained, all site leadership team members must speak with "one voice." The fourth key to a lean business transformation is change leadership. Its four aspects are shown in the table below.

Problem to Solve	Key	What Leaders Do	Leadership Challenge
Conflicting leader visions/ philosophies disrupt lean startups	Change leadership	Leadership work with the mind of a change leader	Encourage the heart

If you Google "leadership," how many hits will you get? Think many millions. Considering that, what can we say about leadership for sure? Only that there's both a lot of interest and a lot of confusion out there. We all know leadership when we see it or feel it, but in words, not so much.

Change leadership, as described herein, isn't "strategic leadership," which sets a corporate direction; nor is it "technology leadership" or "thought leadership," intelligence that defines product innovations or new technical discoveries. It's not so called "lean leadership," which suggests implementing lean tools and systems in an operation; nor is it inspirational leadership aimed at "motivation" or "change management." As defined here, a change leader accepts the strategic direction set by "higher ups" and engages people in the work of organizational transformation, that is, she does the work of change leadership with the mind of a leader.

The Work of Change Leadership

Coauthors Jeffrey Liker and Karyn Ross describe the challenge of organizational transformation this way: "The truth of complex systems is that there is no one best way and no single best practice good for all circumstances. In fact, what we need to learn is how to find our own way – how to become thinking, learning organizations."[4] Yet, while there is surely no specific recipe of changes that can transform an existing business into a lean operation, the systems model in Figure 7.1 defines the work of a change leader.

The Enneagram is an ancient systems model that was brought to Europe from the Middle East by the mystic teacher G. I. Gurdjieff and was

Figure 7.1 The Enneagram of lean transformation.

later published by his student, John. G. Bennett.[5] It has recently been adapted in models and books for pop-psychology fun, but it was originally a framework to guide a process of transformation. Change leaders can use the Enneagram to develop a strategy for lean transformation for a unique operation or value stream, and it defines their work. Below, in brief, are a few milestones on the way to a lean transformation.

Change Leaders Set Direction, Vision, Strategy, and Goals

Business executives examine a business's strengths, weaknesses, opportunities, and threats and then refresh a strategic direction for their various product lines. Operations executives and their managers can then translate their direction into a vision, strategy, and goals.

Companies have long embraced the need for operations leaders to set out a vision, one that supports an executive strategy. Yet the term "vision" can be confusing because it can represent any future projection made by any authority figure, about any aspect of an organization.

A typical vision statement is sometimes just a reworded mission statement, such as "Our vision is to provide the highest quality software that accesses all legal databases." It may just reflect a specific goal, such as "Our vision is to achieve a 20 percent return on investment." A vision could represent a strategic goal like: "We will leverage our technology to become the market leader in Asia." Each of these aspirations might describe a desirable future, yet none provide an operational vision that can focus the efforts of change leaders. Think of an operational vision as what you would see if you took the roof off an ideal production facility or value stream flow at a defined future time.

The operational vision framework in Figure 7.2[6] was sketched after a lengthy dialogue among a Tennessee factory leadership team. It described a just-in-time pull system, hourly-paced material flow and goals of:

- A target metric for equipment: operating equipment effectiveness (OEE) – 85 percent
- A target quality metric: parts made to specification the first-time-through (FTT) – 87 percent
- A target metric for a smoothing flow: every product every interval (EPEI) – 100 percent

Starting a lean transformation requires care, because project setbacks damage the credibility of the effort. So before beginning a change, leaders should anticipate potential disruptions that might impede progress. For example, typical events that might disrupt progress, include: business strategy changes; entering new markets; launching a vital new product; planning for organizational restructuring; installing new production technology or enterprise information systems; conflict among corporate executives, serious challenges from unions, unreliable suppliers; and many others. That's a lot to consider, and some of these issues may be "showstoppers," that is, they

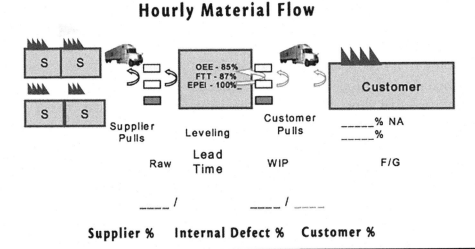

Figure 7.2 An operational vision.

need to be understood because they bring a high risk of failure and sometimes change leaders might best wait to start a lean change until later. Yet once the path forward is clear, or clear enough, they can draft a transformation strategy.

Change Leaders Draft a Transformation Strategy

The Enneagram consists of nine milestones for change around the circumference of a circle, with each one having two inner connections to other points across the circle. These inner connections suggest questions for leaders to consider as they plan change for the future or check back to assure alignment with two previous milestones. The model assumes that process disruptions typically occur at points three, six, and nine, and when they stall or stop progress, change leaders must intervene to enable movement to resume.[7]

A strategy can be drafted by customizing the generic milestones described in Enneagram steps one through nine below, plus discussing each of the two questions derived from two inner connections. (You can review an abbreviated description of these steps in a retrospective from the Tennessee plant in Appendix 1.)

1.0 An executive sets direction and operational leaders draft a vision, strategy, principles, and goals for a lean transformation. Ask: What statements of direction we need? Connections to other points to consider are:

    1.1 Look forward to the fourth milestone and ask which value streams should change?

    1.2 Look forward to the seventh milestone and ask which leadership behaviors and management systems will need to change in order to sustain the vision?

2.0 All leaders volunteer to do an improvement practice, an immersion in a problem-solving group, a process experiment or lean coaching in order to change their basic thinking about leadership and how successful change happens and lasts. Ask: How and when will we get our managers to engage in immersive learning? Connections to other points to consider are:

    2.1 Look forward to the fourth milestone and ask which leaders should lead projects in targeted value streams?

2.2 Look forward to the eighth milestone and ask which individual change leaders should be developed as a sensei?

3.0 Leaders anticipate which key individuals will likely resist change or even disrupt progress. Ask: How can we orient, train, and involve the potential resistors of change? Connections to other points to consider are:

3.1 Look forward to the sixth milestone and ask what possible disruptions may occur?

3.2 Look forward to the ninth milestone and ask when and with whom a sensei should become involved?

4.0 Define value stream strategies and plans for developing people. Ask: What are the likely obstacles on the path to transform each value stream, and plan to counter them? Plus how will we develop people who can and will sustain effective changes? Connections to other points to consider are:

4.1 Look back to the first milestone and ask if progress in targeted value streams reflects the direction, vision, principles, and goals?

4.2 Look back to the second milestone and ask if current actions integrate leaders into a practice, immersion, or experiment?

5.0 Coach rapid improvement events in target areas. Ask: Which value streams can utilize kaizen events or coaching targets in order to hit milestones in the Enneagram plan? Connections to other points to consider are:

5.1 Look forward to the seventh milestone and ask which management systems and leader behaviors will need to change in targeted value streams?

5.2 Look forward to the eighth milestone and ask which proven change leaders can be sensei for new aspiring leaders?

6.0 Leaders respond to disruptions and value stream setbacks. Ask: What are the root causes of the setbacks or delays in our change efforts? Connections to other points to consider are:

6.1 Look forward to the ninth milestone and ask where and when to involve a sensei?

6.2 Look back to the third milestone and ask if resistant individuals have changed? (Consider new options as needed.)

7.0 Align leadership behaviors and management systems to support new lean value streams. Ask: What behaviors or systems will likely be constraints to successful lean value streams? Connections to other points to consider are:

7.1 Look back to the first milestone and ask if new leadership behaviors and management systems compliment the direction, vision, strategy, principles?

7.2 Look back to the fifth milestone and ask if coaches are aligning leadership behaviors and management systems during change?

8.0 Change leaders develop others in the Sensei Way. Ask: Which change leaders could sensei for others? Connections to other points to consider are:

8.1 Look back to the fifth milestone and ask: Which rapid improvement events best served to develop new leaders?

8.2 Look back to the second milestone and ask if practices, immersions, or experiments developed change leaders

9.0 Start a next round of lean learning with a new facility or value stream managers; find a sensei for them. Ask: What do the next set of managers need to learn and who will be the sensei for them? Connections to other points to consider are:

9.1 Look forward to the third milestone and ask which key individuals are likely to resist learning?

9.2 Look forward to the sixth milestone and discuss how to prepare coaches to lead rapid improvement events?

While no strategy or plan will ever be complete or foolproof, a good planning process can build a leadership team's consensus and a response-ability to counter disruptions when they arise during organizational change, as they will. As president Dwight Eisenhower said, "Planning is everything, the plan is nothing."[8]

Change Leaders Do a Practice, Immersion, or Experiment to Change Basic Thinking

Operational leaders provide the basic thinking, that is, the leadership vision, values and a set of operating principles that form the foundation of an organization and its leadership and management approaches. Next, all operations managers need to be immersed in change through participation in improvement events, including kaizen blitzes, value stream mapping, and lean coaching in order to change their basic thinking about how change leadership works and how lean operations can be sustained.

Values are high-level statements about the worth of something and their underlying principles are guidelines for action that support them. For example, if an operation has a value for safety, a corresponding operating principle might be always wearing personal protective equipment (PPE) in a work area. Over the past few decades, it has become common for big enterprises to post a set of values on conference room walls, print them in annual reports, and present them in all-employee meetings.

In the 21st century, most Western business managers have replaced the default industrial-age values of command and control with the more politically correct 21st-century values of "pragmatism" and "empiricism." Pragmatic managers contend that the only meaningful test of any principle, decision, or action is how well it produces a desired result. An empiricist manager wants direct proof prior to making any change and believes that metrics are always necessary to solve problems.[9] However pragmatic-empiricist managers may not be successful in leading an enterprise in the long run. Consider the example of Jack Welch, once the CEO of General Electric (GE) and a manager who was publicized as the ideal corporate leadership role model in the 20th century.

Chief Welsh was nicknamed "Neutron Jack" because he managed by the numbers and at times made deep payroll cuts that left production facilities and offices virtually empty. He used empiricism to force-rank managers and subsequently fired the bottom 10 percent every year. He was so pragmatic that he sold off any GE business unit that wasn't number one or two in its market. Under him, the company is reputed to have become an imperial and financialized empire. Mr. Welsh's leadership values of pragmatism and empiricism were not enough to sustain General Electric as an elite corporation. When the global financial crisis arrived, it devastated its balance sheet and credit rating. Its capitalization went from about 600 billion dollars to roughly 65 billion, and considering future potential exposures, its value could be less than zero.[10] Contrast Mr. Welsh's 20th century values with the Toyota Way 2001 values, as published at the start of the 21st century, as shown in Figure 7.3.

In contrast to narrow pragmatism and empiricism, author Jeffrey Liker summarizes the Toyota 2001 values this way:

> Continuous improvement has three foundational principles – clarify and face the challenge even when it is seemingly impossible, go and see the current reality without preconceptions (genchi genbutsu), and relentless kaizen which means start experimenting, rapidly and scientifically. Respect for people means getting knowledgeable people to work as a team (teamwork) and respecting them all the time motivates them to contribute.

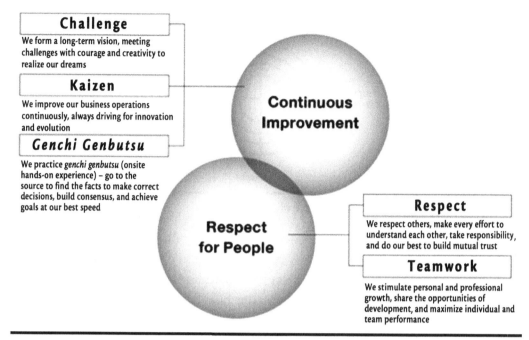

Figure 7.3   Toyota Way 2001 values and principles.

He concludes: "If there is a recipe for Toyota's success, it is a deep, time-consuming, and expensive investment in developing everyone in the organization, and truly believing that your employees are your most precious resource."[11]

Of course, most Western business people abhor talking about philosophy and values, yet conflict among executives and functional managers is often a big reason why new lean work startups stall, lack quick support, and are eventually abandoned or become a "dead man walking."

During a change, many managers will have values at variance with those that sustain a lean operation. Rather than just hoping and wishing that they would adopt new values, a more productive path is to engage them in a radar chart exercise aimed to develop a consensus on leadership's future operating principles. Then, when business and functional managers hold each other accountable to principles, a change in behavior will lead to better results, and only then will the pragmatic-empiricists shift their values to those similar to the Toyota Way.

The radar chart exercise defines two axes that set up four categories of principles. I commonly use the four terms: process, problem solving, people and partners, and philosophy. The four concentric circles in Figure 7.4 indicate four increments of strength, that is, one, three, five, and seven, a seven-point scale.

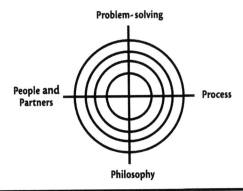

Figure 7.4 Operating principles radar chart.

In the radar chart exercise each functional leader rates an operation's "current state" on each of the categories from one to seven, and the facilitator plots each rating at the appropriate point on the related axis on an easel. After each member places a rating on all four axes, the facilitator briefly inquires about the reasoning or evidence behind a posted number. After posting all team members ratings on each of the four categories, the facilitator then highlights the biggest "gaps" between two individual's ratings. The facilitator then asks one or two pairs with divergent ratings to give additional evidence and examples to justify their current-state numerical rating.

However, a full team consensus on the "current state" on each operating principle isn't the point. Rather, more important is reaching a consensus on the question of: "What should our consensus rating be for each category in our future state?" The aim of a facilitator is to structure a dialogue and enable business or site leaders to reach a consensus on future operating principles in the value stream or operation. Why so? It's vital that after a series of meetings, they all speak with "one voice." Below is an example of a radar chart exercise with a leadership team in a manufacturing plant. The facilitated discussion succeeded in aligning two key managers on a principle that integrated product quality (process axis) and employee empowerment (people axis).

> At the engine plant, Don was a traditional plant manager who spent most of his time firefighting daily problems in production and about quality. During the radar chart exercise, one issue raised was on product quality. During a recent week, engines with a defective part had been shipped to the customer and they had to be fixed in the field. Mike, who was the production manager over the area where the defect originated had long favored empowering teams to check their own work on the line. Given the recent

quality incident, Don disagreed. In the radar chart dialogue, they diverged on their radar chart ratings on the people principle of empowerment. After they debated for a time, the facilitator drafted a quality principle that they both could support. It specified that the company would empower shop floor teams only after quality training and certification of employees was complete.

Change Leaders Coach Rapid Improvement Events in Target Areas

Once strategies have been drafted for all service or product value streams, plus plans for developing people, rapid improvement events and continuous improvement coaching targets initiate a change. When disruptions to progress arise, which they will, leaders must intervene to implement countermeasures or adjust the milestones on the road to a lean business transformation.

Change Leaders Align Leadership Behaviors and Management Systems

The adjustment of leadership behaviors and redesign of management systems is within the purview of an operating executive or a leadership team. Typically, all managers must shift their command and control behaviors to a lean coaching approach. Feedback on change efforts can better focus priorities for policy and systems changes. Better systems, such as enterprise resources planning (ERP) systems software, can provide real-time data and communications that enable managers, teams, and specialists to be aware of process anomalies or quality defects and respond quickly.

Change Leaders Develop Others in the Sensei Way

Change leaders who achieve mastery in leading rapid improvement events or coaching process improvement may choose to become sensei for a next cohort of aspiring change leaders. Finally, enterprise leaders begin to prepare for a lean startup at a new facility or in a next value stream target. It starts by orienting a new set of operations managers to lean thinking, plus its complimentary leadership philosophy, values, and a standard coaching approach.

Change Leaders Engage Others with Situational Leadership

Late in the 20th century, psychologist Fred E. Fielder and his associates made a startling discovery. In their laboratory experiments, the highest performing group leaders didn't exhibit any specific style, consistent behavior, or even any particular traits. Instead, they found that the best leaders engaged others with a flexible approach, one guided by a number of concurrent factors.[12] Dr. Fielder summarized their critical leadership capability this way: "I shall argue that the active ingredient is the degree to which the situation causes uncertainty and stress and therefore anxiety."[13] There will always be some individuals who resist learning or are anxious about needed changes. Change leaders learn to balance both challenge and respect, using responses that encourage others to become mindful and learn. What does situational leadership look like in action? Former vice president Frank Giannattasio engaged Wiremold's unionized shop floor employees daily with a situational leadership approach. Here's a brief example:

> During our lean implementation there was constant communication with staff groups, line workers, and the union officers. I had to do a lot of talking, and I'd ask, Why can't you try it this way? If it doesn't work, we can put it back. The key to success was stamina, staying with it through many repetitions and never declaring victory.

What is the nature of the flexible, situational mind that executives, managers, and coaches need in order to do the work of change leadership?

The Mind of a Change Leader

Jeffrey Liker writes that the basic thinking of the Toyota Way is, "Literally about resetting the corporate metabolism, DNA."[14] DNA is the material that carries the genes of an organism, so just what are the actual genes that form a change leader's mindset? Rasmus Hougaard and Jacqueline Carter compiled data on 30,000 leaders in *The Mind of a Leader*[15] and described three mental qualities of leaders.[16] Figure 7.5 defines the mind of a change leader in similar but not identical terms.

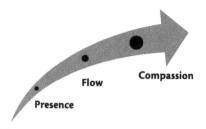

Figure 7.5 The mind of a change leader.

Presence

Presence is a confusing term because it has at least three contemporary meanings. One meaning is "awareness of what is," which is synonymous with mindfulness. Say you're startled by a loud noise from outside on the street, your natural reaction might be to pass judgment such as: "People shouldn't be that noisy in this neighborhood." A mindful response would be to resist any judgment on the source of the sound and ask: "I wonder what the heck that noise was?" Then, upon going outside to check, you might find that the noise arose from a construction job across the street.

A second meaning of presence is living in a way that expresses one's highest aspiration, being one's "best self" and fulfilling one's potential.[17] Say for example, you have musical aptitude, perhaps inherited from a parent. If you were to develop and skillfully display your music talent on the stage, you might well exhibit a "personal presence" during your performance. This second kind of presence can readily segway into the third.

The third meaning of presence is a lucid state of awareness that's the result of both concentration and diminishing self-concern. It harmonizes two aspects of our being: The first is our human "being." It's our internal energy or essence, which is usually buried beneath our constant stream of thoughts, emotions, and activities. In quiet times, we feel our being as a sense of "care."[18] For example, when we hug our children, our parents or relate with our dearest friends, our minds clear, and we feel our being as an inner peace. When this happens our human "being" resonates with a deeper substrait of being.[19]

This deeper or "big" being is a primordial energy, a power that undergirds and fuels all life. Author Eckhart Tolle described it as: "The un-manifested and eternal consciousness."[20]

In a nutshell, when we engage in mindfulness at work or home, it displaces our usual fixed mindset of thoughts and beliefs, our normal default setting. Then presence arises and we awaken to higher consciousness. Once there, we directly perceive that things, people and events arise according to changing causes and conditions in each moment. And we understand that most of those conditions are beyond any individual's immediate control! Yet when we learn to let go of fear and the urge to control, and trust in presence, we become able to act in concert with the continuous unfolding of reality.

When we are present in being, we lead out of a greater bandwidth of consciousness, which delivers us new insights, intuitions, and perhaps even revelations from a higher power. An insight is an understanding of a specific cause and effect within a specific context. An intuition is knowledge without proof, evidence or conscious reasoning, a personal inner knowing, without apparent deliberate rational thought. A revelation comes from Latin, meaning to "lay bare." It is a surprising and previously unknown fact or paradigm, often made known in a dramatic way.[21] Robert Persig describes the value of presence this way: "When you are really stuck in a problem or challenge, it's presence that tells you where you ought to go."[22] Mr. Tolle suggests asking three questions to check and see if you are present:[23]

■ Can you separate your awareness from disappointments?
■ Can you separate your awareness from your own narrative stories about work and life?
■ Can you perceive the spaciousness and the aliveness in the world?

What's the value of presence for a change leader? It brings a personal resilience, a degree of invulnerability that enables staying in flow even when setbacks or conflicts arise at work or in life. Then, rather than being anxious or caught up in worry, a leader can see challenging events as opportunities to help others learn and develop.

Presence has several qualities: immersion in the here and now, a non-dualistic mind, a smooth integration of thoughts, emotions, actions and the senses, and an inner feeling of peace and well-being.

Presence is a state that people readily perceive in a leader's words, eyes, body language, and demeanor, and it can transmute their negative attitudes into commitments to lead change. When a change leader has developed the capacity to stay present in uncertainty and conflict, a second state of being will arise naturally.

Flow

The early Greek philosophers represented flow with the word "enthousiasmos," meaning "filled with Theos," that is, with God.[24] Psychologist Mihaly Csikszentmihalyi defined it at work this way:[25]

> Flow happens when people become so involved in what they are doing that the activity becomes spontaneous, almost automatic; they stop being aware of themselves as separate from the actions they are performing.

Dr. Csikszentmihalyi describes the value of flow as bringing the "opportunity to concentrate," "sufficient control," and "loss of ego."[26] Most of us find flow when we engage in activities that we find intrinsically rewarding, be they a favorite art or craft, a sport, gardening, building or fixing things, in conversation, doing math proofs, and solving the challenges of software coding, etc. We may call the feeling of flow a "high," "being with it," "grooving," "just doin' it," "jazzin," or "playing in the zone." We all know it when we're in it, because we sense that we're playing or doing our best, even though we aren't judging ourselves with our intellect.

But there's a catch.

Due to our human emotions, instincts, drives, and our frequently agitated minds, virtually no one can stay present and be in flow all the time. Flow requires first sustaining presence, which in turn, relies on maintaining good physical health, a healthy diet, exercising, authentic relationships, adequate rest, and self-care.[27] Sustaining flow also requires maintaining a psychological balance inside one's own self.

How can that be accomplished?

Staying in balance is analogous to the adjustments made by the captain of a sailboat. A captain leads by sensing the interactions of many forces including the wind, the rudder, the tension between the ropes and the sail, plus the actions of the crew, and responds in a way that maintains a balance among them, or evokes a needed shift in direction. Similarly, change leaders must sense the different needs of customers, bosses and functional groups, plus feel the tugs and pulls of their own inner thoughts and feelings and act in ways that maintain balance or evoke a change that creates progress. Author Michael A. Singer has described how to stay in a personal psychological balance this way:

You move from balance point to balance point, from center to center. You can't have any concepts or preferences; you have to let the forces move you. In this way, nothing is personal. You are merely an instrument in the hands of the forces, participating in a harmony of balance.

Staying in flow enables a leader to work sequentially and engage others in ways that accomplish more than was previously thought possible.

Flow is a leader's superpower.

Finally, when a change leader can stay present and work in flow, she will witness others as they struggle with waste in their jobs and in conflicts with their bosses or coworkers, yet do their best. Then, a third state of being will arise in the consciousness of a leader.

Compassion

In the 19th century, German philosophers defined Einfuhlung, as "in-feeling," which was translated into English as "empathy" in 1909. It was described as a "mingling" one's consciousness with that of another. These days we might say that empathy is opening one's self to perceive the mind of another person, to resonate with their inner thoughts and feelings.

That's the good news. However, the bad news is that it can cloud a leader's judgment. Paul Bloom, the author of *Against Empathy*, differentiates compassion from empathy this way: "Compassion means I give your concern weight, I value it. I care about you, but I don't necessarily pick up your feelings."[28] When a change leader can stay present, find flow, and be compassionate, altruism arises naturally. Altruism is a concern for the happiness and success of others, and it uplifts peoples" spirits and draws them forward. As illustrated in Figure 7.6, exercising the capacity for altruism, a change leader encourages the heart.[29]

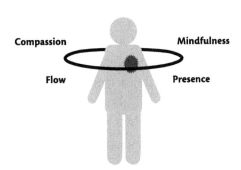

Figure 7.6   A virtuous circle of altruism.

Reflection: What Can We Learn from Change Leadership?

Change leaders aren't successful due to any style, trait, or behavior, nor are they effective by trying to directly influence employees with their personality or inspirational speeches. They succeed by doing the work of change with the mind of a leader. Question is, who can develop this state of mind in an aspiring leader?

What You Can Do

Contract with a sensei or mentor and begin leading change projects in your business operation. Periodically reflect and dialogue with your teacher on progress and setbacks in order to learn how to start and sustain lean operations, plus its complimentary leadership philosophy and coaching practice. At some point, you may become a sensei for other, new aspiring leaders.

Notes

1 *A New Earth*, by Eckhart Tolle, Plume by the Penguin Group, 2005, p. 210.
2 *Flow*, Mihaly Csikszentmihaly, Harper Perennial, 1990, p. 56.
3 *Beyond Religion, Ethics for a Whole World, His Holiness the Dalai Lama*, Mariner Books, Houghton Mifflin Harcourt, 2011, p. 45.
4 *The Toyota Way to Service Excellence*, Jeffrey K. Liker and Karyn Ross, McGraw Hill Education, 2019, p. 81.
5 *The Dramatic Universe*, Volume III, J. G. Bennett, Claymont Communications, 1966, p. 63–72.
6 A plant leadership team that drafted this vision and unified their commitment to it after much debate.
7 *The Dramatic Universe*, Volume III, J. G. Bennett, Claymont Communications, 1966, p. 63.
8 BrainyQuote.com.
9 Google definition of "empiricism."
10 GE Heads Toward Zero, Felix Salmon, Axios, September 3, 2020.
11 *The Toyota Way to Lean Leadership*, Jeffrey K. Liker and Gary L. Convis, McGraw-Hill, 2012, p. 16.
12 Dr. Fiedler's research found that a situational leader changes his or her approach according to a mix of factors, including the degree of task structure, the power and authority of the leader, and favorability of the leader's relationship with an individual or team.
13 *The Leadership Situation and the Black Box Contingency Theories*, Fred E. Fiedler, in Leadership theory and Research, Ed. Martin M. Chemers and Roya Ayman, Academic Press, Harcourt Brace Jovanovich, 1993, p. 2.

14 *The Toyota Way to Lean Leadership*, Jeffrey K. Liker and Gary L. Convis, McGraw-Hill, 2011, p. 8.

15 *The Mind of the Leader*, Rasmus Hougaard and Jacqueline Carter, Harvard Business Review Press, 2018.

16 *The Mind of the Leader*, Rasmus Hougaard and Jacqueline Carter, Harvard Business Review Press, 2018, p. 3.

17 *Presence*, Amy Cuddy, Little Brown Spark, 2015, p. 3.

18 Martin Heidegger described "being in the world" as our human experience when we "care." Being and Time, Martin Heidegger, Martino Fine Books, 2019, Harper and Row, 1962, p. 284.

19 Martin Heidegger described the definition of "being" as "being in the world." His notion was that our human being is experienced when we "care" about something more than ourselves. Being and Time, Martin Heidegger, Martino Fine Books, 2019, Harper and Row, 1962, p. 284.

20 *A New Earth*, Eckhart Tolle, Penguin, 2005, p. 91.

21 Dictionary on-line.

22 *Zen and the Art of Motorcycle Maintenance*, Robert M. Pirsig, Harper Perennial Classics, originally published by William Morrow and Company, 1974, p. 282.

23 *A New Earth*, Eckhart Tolle, Penguin, 2005, p. 177.

24 *Zen and the Art of Motorcycle Maintenance*, Robert M. Pirsig, Harper Perennial Classics, originally published by William Morrow and Company, 1974, p. 303.

25 *Flow, Mihaly Csikszentmihalyi, The Psychology of Optimal Experience*, Mihaly Csikszentmihaly, Harper Perennial, 1990, p. 53.

26 *Good Business, Leadership Flow and the Making of Meaning*, Mihaly Csikszentmihalyi, Penguin Books, 2003, p. 131–138.

27 Self-care is doing things to maintain our mental, emotional, and physical health.

28 Cited on the Vox website, Sean Illing, August 20, 2018; Paul Bloom is the author of *Against Empathy, the Case for Rational Compassion*, Harper Collins, 2016.

29 *The Leadership Challenge*, James M. Kouzes and Barry Z. Posner, Jossey Bass, 2007.

Chapter 8

The Fifth Key Is the Sensei Way

We say that at Toyota, every leader is a teacher developing the next generation of leaders. This is their most important job.[1]

Akio Toyoda

The life in our heads, the life we think is our life, is not our real life. We should not mix them up.[2]

Taizan Maezumi Roshi

AT THE TENNESSEE PLANT'S CUSTOMER

A compatriot and leadership sensei, Tom Lane, was asked to give a half-hour talk to executives at the Tennessee plant's automotive customer in Detroit. Their corporate quality leader had asked him to speak to the CEO and his executive team on: What it takes to achieve quality at the level of Toyota? Below his recollection of the meeting.[3]

Since I only had 30 minutes to speak to the CEO and his team, I didn't want to fill the time with me talking. So, I did something more intuitive. I wrote the terms "process" and "systems thinking" on an easel at the front of the conference room. I wanted them to consider the two ideas, which I knew were related to quality, and invited them to speak. I just asked, What do you think?

The CEO pondered the words for a minute. Then, he said that earlier in his career, when he was at Ford in Europe, process was how they figured out the flow of parts and cars. He said that they hadn't used the term back then, but that they knew how it worked. In my reply, I related process thinking to systems thinking, and we dialogued for five minutes on how the two concepts were complimentary. Then, I turned to the head of vehicle design and asked: do you need to do systems thinking during design work. Of course, he replied. He proceeded to cite the numerous factors involved in designing a car. Next, the two executives spontaneously began a dialogue relating car design to factory design. They had a great 20-minute talk. I just stayed present and flowed along with their conversation, asking questions now and then to spur more discussion.

Finally to conclude things I asked them: How do process and systems thinking apply to running a big corporation like yours? The question prompted a long and enlightening dialogue that generated a positive feeling in the room. It was sort of magical. At that point, everyone understood that they had to work together for the company to be a success. Afterward, the cooperate quality leader told me that it was the best conversation anyone had ever seen them have. I was willing to let the executives take the lead and just listening and supporting their dialogue. Trust in my ability to stay present was the key.

During Tom's conversation with the top executives, they entered into a state of flow in communication, and it strengthened their relationship, at least for a time.

However, when business executives or site leadership team members can't stay present during discord with their peers, they push conflict down to their middle managers who then often fail to deliver timely support for lean startups. In order for them to learn how to stay present in uncertainty and conflict, most will need the mentoring of a sensei. So the fifth and final key to starting and sustaining a lean transformation in a Western business is the Sensei Way. Its four aspects are shown in the table below.

Problem to Solve	Key	What Leaders Do	Leadership Challenge
How leaders can learn to stay present in uncertainty and conflict	The Sensei Way	Realize and do the one big thing	Model the way

The Sensei Way

The Japanese term sensei generally means "teacher" and literally, "one who has gone before."[4] Where has a sensei gone before? A sensei has gone deep into immersion in a challenge with no possibility of escape, and realized the way. Author Ray Grigg describes the value of such Zen experience this way:[5]

> Zen's essential subject is how is a person to act within perpetual change and uncertainty, between what is and what will be. The obvious answer was to anticipate the changes by attempting to read the movement of circumstances, and then change them, avoid them, or be prepared for them.

Mr. Grigg's description is an excellent working definition of change leadership! Figure 8.1 describes how a sensei develops the mind of a change leader. Why does an aspiring change leader require a sensei? One Zen teacher described our fundamental human problem this way:[10] "Most of us, most of the time are skipping through the world without awareness. We see people and things not as they are, but as we are, because our minds limit new perceptions and insights." In my decades of executive coaching, I began each visit to a client with what I called a "learning conversation."

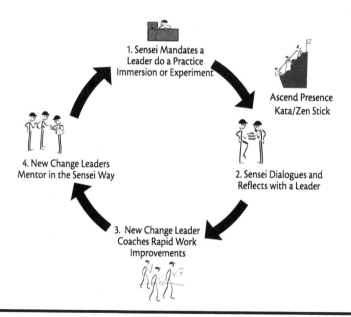

1. Sensei Mandates a Leader do a Practice Immersion or Experiment

Ascend Presence Kata/Zen Stick

2. Sensei Dialogues and Reflects with a Leader

3. New Change Leader Coaches Rapid Work Improvements

4. New Change Leaders Mentor in the Sensei Way

Figure 8.1   The Sensei Way. Leapers © Copyright, *Lean Enterprise Institute, Inc.,* All rights reserved. Lean Enterprise Institute, the leaper image, and stick figure image are registered trademarks of *Lean Enterprise Institute, Inc.,* Used with permission.

It was based on the gestalt psychology idea that raising awareness alone can enable new learning. However, a sensei doesn't employ psychology but rather engages an aspiring leader in Zen experience. Roshi Philip Kapleau described the three aims of a sensei's teaching: the first is establishing "concentration"; the second is "realizing the way"; the third is "living the way"; and to Kapleau's list, I'll add a fourth aim of "teaching the way."

1. The Sensei Mandates that a Leader Do a Practice, Immersion, or Experiment

    In the first stage of the Sensei Way, the teacher aims to increase an aspiring leader's ability to concentrate, that is, to be singularly focused on what is happening in real time.

    The teacher knows that our human thinking is egoistic, and that such thinking will usually be a misfit and thus unable to resolve new arising challenges and compound problems, especially those involving people and culture. So in periodic dialogue and reflection, a sensei will use various tactics to increase a leader's concentration, awareness in the now. The authors of *The Lean Sensei* describe several initial tactics that a sensei might employ to increase a leader's concentration.[6]

    – Challenge a leader's discipline: They could point at places in the workplace where things aren't happening as they should, yet offer no help, no ready answers, and no advice.
    – Give a leader exercises: They would narrow down on one area, without explaining why, and then assign a task to do.
    – Give a leader undivided attention: They would seldom validate, agree, or encourage, but they would listen patiently to justifications, doubt, issues, impossibilities, and completely ignore what other operational drama was happening.
    – Push a leader to take the next step: They were always demanding more, further, beyond.

    Next, aiming to strengthen concentration, a sensei mandates that a leader enter into immersion in problem solving, participate in a kaizen event or a work redesign experiment, or coach an individual or team as they work to improve their work and systems.[7] Immersion brings a productive tension which strengthens what Buddhists call joriki in a leader's mindset, meaning "self-power." It is a mind unified and brought to one-pointedness.[8]

    Inevitable distractions compete for attention and often trigger agitated thinking and random activity by a leader, what does a sensei do to bring her back to presence in the moment.

2. The Sensei Dialogues and Reflects with the Leader

In the second stage of the Sensei Way, the teacher's goal is to help the leader realize the way, that is, to awaken from the dominance of egoistic mind and discover what Buddhists call shinjin.[9] It is to grasp in the depth of one's consciousness how things actually are. And how are they? Continuously changing, interrelated, and insubstantial, including each one of us ourselves.

Western reason and science have led to new technologies, making modern life easier. However, an unfortunate side effect of the highly rational focus in Western education and business has legitimized and exploded our human habit of excess thinking. As a result, most of us are stuck in our own ongoing chain of thoughts, what the Buddhists call "monkey mind." At the center, driving our excessive thinking is the ego, a fictional self we believe in,[10] and it constantly asserts and defends our impulses, emotions and biased stories at work and in life.

Coauthors Hougaard and Carter list several downsides of the ego: ego makes you vulnerable to criticism; ego makes you susceptible to manipulation; ego narrows your field of vision; and ego corrupts your behavior and causes you to act against your values.[11] Finally, and perhaps most significantly, egoistic thinking obstructs a leader's mindfulness, which is the doorway to the state of presence. We all have embarrassing moments when our behavior is hijacked by our ego, and below is an embarrassing story of the time a corporate executive taught me a lesson.

As a new corporate consultant, I was thrilled to join 50 or so executives, managers, and consultants at a systems thinking workshop. On the first evening, I was invited for dinner with a group of senior executives and consultants from big U.S. companies like DuPont and AT&T. Midway through the meal, I became overly-excited and launched into a lecture about how that day's learning was great and how it might transform their companies. As I dominated the conversation around the table, I felt an inner glow of self-pride. I did have a passing thought that perhaps I was talking too much, but I ignored it. There was no response to my speech from the executives around the table the conversation just moved on. After dinner, I was walking to my car in the parking lot when the AT&T executive came up and asked: What was the purpose of your long monologue during dinner? I thought a few seconds, couldn't come up with one, and I honestly replied: I'm not sure. He paused a moment for emphasis then finished with: That's what I thought.

Similar to that AT&T exec, a sensei will at times challenge a leader to learn from direct, painful experience. Lean coach David Verble suggests several initial questions to ask a leader during reflection: (1) What did you do compared to what you intended to do? (2) What was the response versus what you expected? (3) Why do you think the response was the same or different from what you expected? (4) What did you learn from how the other person or people reacted? (5) What will you do the same or differently next time?

Next a sensei might choose to challenge a leader to review a problem or an improvement project in a shop, lab, or office, in order to test the validity of her thoughts, approach, or proposed solutions. Third, like a Japanese sensei, a teacher might diminish a leader's ego with a non-rational response. A few I've witnessed in the past are: Saying nothing in response to a question; using an ambiguous response like grunting, sighing, or shrugging; conveying a look that expresses doubt or rejection; making a facial expression that communicates an authentic attitude; expressing a blunt, not-politically correct comment or question; using negative body language, head shaking; just walking away; or looking amused as if by silliness.

The sensei uses reflection and dialogue about recent experiences in change projects to stimulate learning about how sustainable change happens. Reflection on events and especially disappointments and mishaps can help a leader renounce an egoistic mindset and habitual behaviors, and ultimately choose to make mindfulness her default state of mind.

The sensei's psychological lessons for an aspiring leader are four-fold. The first is that: "You are not your thoughts." Normally, most of us identify with our thoughts, beliefs, our mindset, so strongly that we lose self-awareness, and our "identification" with it leads people to lose mindfulness and we "become" our thoughts. As a result, most assert or defend their thoughts aggressively and irrationally. The second lesson is the realization that: "Thoughts are not real." In reflecting on a thought for a time, it morphs or dissipates, and a leader can realize that no thought is solid, that all are ephemeral. When a leader can separate unreal thoughts from real events, she can consider situations freely, objectively and creatively. Third, transformational learning strikes when a leader gains the real-time skill to consider thoughts, compartmentalize them for later, or just let them go. Fourth, by grasping the ephemeral nature of thinking, leaders can choose to make mindfulness their default mindset, and to quickly become present when uncertainty or conflict arise. Then in presence, a leader will experience a state of inner peace and equanimity, even in challenging situations.

Eckhart Tolle writes that: "Presence doesn't transform 'what is' directly, it transforms you."[12] How so? One change leader reported that after working with a sensei she felt invisible, but in a "good way." Presence brings a leader what the Buddhists call tariki or "other power." It's what Mr. Tolle called: "the power of now," which he described this way:

> When you are fully present and people around you manifest unconscious behavior, you won't feel the need to react to it, so you don't give it any reality. Your peace is so vast and deep that anything that is not peace disappears into it as if it had never existed. This breaks the karmic circle of action and reaction.

Presence gives leaders resilience and the power to reconcile personal and organizational conflicts.

3. New Change Leaders Coach Rapid Work Improvements

In this third stage of the Sensei Way, the teacher mandates that a leader lead a series of rapid improvement events so that she will learn to "live the way," that is, develop the ability to stay present and work in a state of flow during change projects. In this step a sensei might challenge a leader's over confidence with numerous difficult questions, so that she will let go of reliance on old paradigms, beliefs, and habits. Then, for a time, a change leader will to "live the way," that is, engage work and people in presence and flow, knowing that insight and intuition will arise when needed, just in time. Mr. Tolle puts it this way: "Instead of asserting one's will or reacting against a situation, you become present and merge with it, and then a solution will arise out of the situation itself."[13]

A sensei may recycle an aspiring change leader through these first three stages of the Sensei Way until she can be mindful of situations, stay present despite uncertainty and conflict, and frequently enter into a fluid state of flow in working or communicating during change efforts. What might a change leader do then?

4. New Change Leaders Mentor Others in the Sensei Way

In the fourth stage of the Sensei Way, the proven change leader has received personal "transmission" from the sensei and begins to "teach the way." That is, she begins to guide a new individual or cohort of aspiring leaders through the four stages. Below are the recollections of Mike Funke, a compatriot and a manager who was early-on engaged with Japanese sensei, later became a change leader, became an executive and finally a sensei for others.[14]

Early in my career my job was as a factory production planner and I was passionate about making things better. I had already read every book on lean production, gone to conferences, and learned all I could on my own, and so I was happy when my company hired a Toyota sensei. My early involvement with him was a bit of a shock, and it taught me a new way to think and improve the work. The sensei's coaching was intense but respectful. He had high expectations and focused on data and an observation-driven problem-solving methodology, plus taking immediate action as well. He asked a lot of questions, rarely answered any, and would use curt statements such as "please try now," which basically meant that discussion time was over. Again, even this reinforced the iterative, kaizen mentality, which is to use 5-Why thinking to diagnose the root causes of waste, make changes on the fly, check the results and do it again.

There were three lessons I took away from the time with my sensei: First, if you engage a focused and purposeful team, they can accomplish amazing things, more than you ever dreamed possible. Second, a challenge from a sensei is essential to stretch and get to the best work design or quality solution that's possible. Third, after you achieve success, you must seek out and resolve the next obstacle with as much vigor as the first; it never ends! The sensei didn't tell us this, but he did teach it to us. The sensei's demanding way of coaching transformed my approach as a problem solver, coach, and leader.

Throughout my career I have immersed my staff and others in coaching experiences and served as a second coach when they began coaching on their own. They soon grasped the fundamentals of being mindful, finding waste, problem solving to root causes and doing rapid improvement cycles. The experience has served them throughout their careers, and I still interact with them at times. They have now become mentors for a new set of rising leaders. As a teacher, I have had the joy and privilege of touching many lives and hopefully making their career experience more challenging and fulfilling. I am very proud of that.

When an aspiring leader avoids immersion or backslides a sensei might strike her with a business version of the Zen stick.

Speak Softly and Carry a Zen Stick

In the Zendo, a meditation teacher, called a jikijitsu, will at times, strike a daydreaming or dozing meditator on with a thin, flat stick. It's known as a kyosaku (or a keisaku in some schools), but is commonly called the Zen stick.[15] While it's best for a sensei to be respectful of others, there are times when an aspiring business change leader retreats into undisciplined thinking, negative emotions, or bad habits. At these times, a sensei might choose to deliver a "wake-up call" to evoke presence in an aspiring leader. Here's a story of a time when Toyota's Sensei Ohno struck a supervisor with the Zen stick.[16]

> I was at the Takaoka Plant the other day. They had body shells hanging from the overhead conveyor in the paint shop. I told the general manager, he had too much work-in-process and instructed him to reduce the volume.
>
> We'll get right on it, he said. Just give us a little time.
>
> I went back after a couple of hours and asked, Have you taken care of the excess work-in-process?
>
> We'll get it done this Saturday, he said.
>
> Fine, I said. In the meantime, I'm going to trash all these body shells hanging here. Get me a ladder and a hammer now!
>
> The general manager agreed to get the job done right away.

What does striking with the Zen stick look like during a kaizen event? Here's an example.[17]

My lean event sponsor was an engineering manager and right away he explained that his aim was for the kaizen team to review the engineering department's plan to modify assembly line, to work out the "bugs."

I told him: We're not going to do that. We're going to follow the kaizen principles and process.

The engineering manager looked disappointed, shook his head, and walked away.

During the lean event, I had the team collect data on job times, yield, quality defects, and job elements and identify process waste at each work station. Then, they brainstormed ways to redesign the work to eliminate the waste in the line. At one point, a welder from the second shift spoke on a kaizen idea saying: If the initial workstation could just tack weld all attached parts to the vehicle frame accurately, then the second work station could be 'heads down' in efficient, uninterrupted welding of all final components.

The team agreed that the idea eliminated time at the first work station and thus would allow managers to assign less experienced welders to the initial tack weld and senior welder at the second station would do the final weld, a change that would produce more consistent quality. The new work design consolidated and simplified raw parts delivery as well. At the end of the kaizen event, the engineering manager told me: Thanks for not doing what I asked you to do.

A sensei or change leader should show all people respect, yet when facing a bully, a cheat, or a liar, striking with the Zen stick may be the best choice in a difficult moment. Here's a time when I had a mandate from a vice president to train and facilitate a design team for a new plant, a time when I chose to strike a design team leader with the Zen stick. Please don't try this at home.

I was assigned by a vice president to coach a team of American and French engineers who were making a factory plan for a new plant in France. He told me to teach them about u-shaped work cells, flexible, cross-trained employees, minimal staffing and empowered teams. A final design review of the first line was scheduled with the VP and his peers at the corporate offices three months later.

When I arrived onsite for my first visit, I reviewed the design team leader's initial production line blue print. It was, predictably, a traditional mass-production line, with short-cycle time jobs and product quality to be checked through sampling by a staff group. During that first week, I oriented the design team to u-shaped work cells, empowered teams with cross-training for all jobs, just-in-time materials delivery and kaizen. At the start of the second week, I arranged a speaker-phone call with an experienced work cell manager, and the design team became enthusiastic. At the end of that week, they had designed a u-shaped cell on a blueprint, calculated its staffing, located materials staging, and defined needed training for the first production team. I returned home feeling that success was in the offing. However, when I returned for the third and final visit, the plan had been changed. I arrived near lunch time on a Monday morning, took a seat in an upstairs conference room, and slipped my shoes off under the table. The design team leader was reviewing a blue print taped to an easel up front, one identical with the original layout that he the team lead had presented in our first meeting two months before. I stopped him immediately and ask: What's this? I thought the team agreed on a u-shaped work cell last time?

Well, he said, I reviewed our plan with my boss. He told me that since we don't know what kind of space the second line will need, in order to secure maximum space for use later, we'll use the straight line for the first one. We might do a work cell on the next one.

A tense silence descended over the conference room. I paused to slip on my loafers beneath the conference room table, slowly stood up, and walked to the front of the room. The team leader was frozen in place standing next to the easel. I didn't feel angry, I just felt an inner sense of "no." After a few moments standing up front an intuition arose. I picked up the easel, carefully carried it out of the second-floor conference room door, took a few additional steps, and dropped it down the stairs. As it crashed down to the landing below, its legs broke off and the blue prints scattered. I followed it down and walked to the cafeteria for lunch. During lunch time, the design team leader approached me cautiously and said:

I talked to my boss and he said that we'll go back to the work cell design and team concept when we present the plan at the meeting for the VP's approval.

I'll be there. I replied. I left to go home after lunch.

Of course, this kind of intuitive response could have gotten me fired if I hadn't had the full sponsorship of the operations vice president. Former Toyota coach David Verble worked with a future Toyota CEO, Fujio Cho, during his time working in Kentucky. He recently described how Mr. Cho used questions rather than a Zen stick.[18]

> Ohno had a reputation for having been rather heavy-handed (to all levels) in his efforts to try out and improve Toyota-style production tools and practices. I only experienced that a few times from sensei who were his disciples. I have worked with and been coached by several Toyota sensei in Japan and the US. What I got from the others who were trying to coach and develop me (even when they were frustrated with my slow learning curve) were questions. Many, many open-ended questions, such as Why do you say that? What have you seen? How do you know? Why do you think that? What is the problem? What is the purpose? What is the cause? What is the plan? What did you expect? What happened? What do you think now? At some point, I finally realized the purpose of those questions was to make me set aside assumptions, see and think about what was really happening.

Please note that in our Western corporate culture, striking someone with the Zen stick will be considered politically incorrect, could damage a relationship, and might even be a firing offense. So please don't strike with the Zen stick anytime soon. When you're wise enough to use it, you won't need to read a book like this.

Reflection: What Can We Learn from the Sensei Way?

When I reflected on what my long-ago Japanese sensei did when I asked him how he was so successful in leading Americans. He smiled and just walked away, but he might well have answered "mu," meaning in Japanese, "no thing". Saying mu would have meant something like: "Don't ask that question because the answer can't be understood in words." Rather than words, a sensei uses immersion in Zen experience to develop change leaders, who then use their intuitive understanding to guide action that is direct, plain, concrete, and highly practical.[19]

In a corporate setting, a lean business transformation requires finding a sensei who can develop a cadre of change leaders through a "direct transmission" of the way via the four stages of the Sensei Way. This cohort of new leaders can become a starter culture, a kind of "Petri dish" for a new philosophy of leadership, one that is compatible with starting and sustaining a lean business transformation.

What You Can Do

Over my years of coaching and leading change, I've developed a DIY model for the Sensei Way. It's a template that's derived from meditation,* and it can help you raise your own consciousness or track a dialogue with another person.[20] It's shown in Figure 8.2.

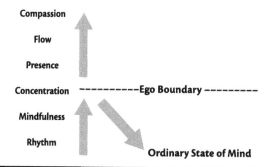

Figure 8.2   The presence kata.

The steps of the presence kata are as follows:

1. Establish a practice or ritual that brings rhythm and focus to the body and stability in the mind. This can be a physical movement, rhythmic breathing, repeating a mantra, doing a visualization, among others.
2. Set aside your own agenda and become a witness, mindful of "what is," in your self and you surroundings without bias, judgment, or obvious projection.
3. In order to strengthen mindfulness, concentrate attention for one minute (30 in and out breaths) on each of the following. First notice the

---

* A complete description of the Wheel of Awareness can be found in Chapter 15, *Mind, Consciousness, and Well-Being*, Edited by Daniel J. Siegel and Marion F. Solomon, W W. Norton and Co., 2020, p. 313.

surroundings, sensing what it sounds like, smells like, looks like, or feels like. Don't do anything with the information, just notice. Next notice bodily sensations of comfort or discomfort for a minute. Now, for another minute, attend to your thoughts and impressions, not judging them, just allowing them pass through and out of your mind. Move through this sequence daily to strengthen mindfulness.

4. Concentrate your attention back onto your own awareness for a minute. When concentration is lost, return attention to your awareness. As you do this, let go of all self-concern and you will enter into the state of presence for a time.

5. Stay present and you will be naturally drawn to a motivating task or a meaningful communication, and as you begin; a flow state will arise.

6. When you stay present engage in flow, you will see people stuck in conflict with others or experiencing suffering due to their own undisciplined minds. Then, compassion will arise naturally within you.

Practice using the presence kata in quiet times, and it will serve you when people, events, or your own thoughts and emotions disrupt your mind. Eventually when you have made mindfulness your default state of mind, you will be able to jump quickly to step 4.

This chapter completes the description of the five keys to a lean business transformation. Yet there is something else change leaders need to understand.

Notes

1 *The Lean Sensei*, Lean Enterprise Institute, 2019, p. 17.
2 *Appreciate Your Life*, Taizan Maezumi Roshi, Shambhala Publications, 2001, p. 17.
3 Story from Thomas R. Lane.
4 Definition given in an email from Jeffrey K. Liker.
5 *The Tao of Zen*, Ray Grigg, Alva Press, 1994, p. 3.
6 *The Lean Sensei*, Lean Enterprise Institute, 2019, p. 25–26.
7 However, the focus would not be on analytical tasks like conceptualizing a business strategy.
8 *The Heart of the Shin Buddhist Path*, Takamaro Shigaraki, Wisdom Publications, 2013, p. 49.
9 *The Heart of the Shin Buddhist Path*, Takamaro Shigaraki, Wisdom Publications, 2013, Chapter 5.

10 MRI scans have found no physical region that's home for a "self" in the brain. Thoughts of "self" are only distributed electrical activity across many parts of the brain.

11 *The Mind of the Leader*, Rasmus Hougaard and Jacqueline Carter, Harvard Business Review Press, 2018, p. 66–70.

12 *The Power of Now*, Eckhart Tolle, New World Library and Namaste Publishing, 1999, p. 217.

13 *A New Earth*, Eckhart Tolle, Penguin, 2005, p. 238.

14 Interview with Mike Funke, now Vice President of Supply Chain, ESCO Corporation.

15 *The Encouragement Stick: 7 Views*, Tricycle Magazine, The Editors, Winter, 1998.

16 *The Birth of Lean*, Koichi Shimokawa and Takahiro Fujimoto, Editors, Lean Enterprise Institute, 2009, p. 32.

17 Story from Kaizen Institute of America consultant and now a vice president, James Van Patton.

18 Interview with David Verble, July 2018.

19 Quote adapted from D. T. Suzuki, in Zen Buddhism: Selected Writings of D. T. Suzuki, Doubleday Anchor Books, William Bennett, editor, 1956, p. 53.

20 The steps in Zen meditation are entering the room and bowing, sitting on and positioning yourself on a cushion, looking forward without focusing much, and finally beginning rhythmic breathing or another focusing ritual. Next is to become mindful of the body's sensations and thoughts and letting them pass out of awareness. By sustaining mindfulness for a time, the ego boundary is passed, and presence displaces it as the default state.

Chapter 9

It's a Wabi Sabi World

Our current modes of rationality are not moving society into a better world.[1]

Robert Persig

Wabi sabi can, in its fullest expression, be a way of life.

Leonard Koren

IN THE TENNESSEE PLANT

The Tennessee plant's transformation was the result of a partnership between two successive plant managers, a UAW leader, a visiting Japanese sensei, his American lean consultants, and a dedicated corporate vice president who set the direction and paid the bills. The plant's once-disengaged workforce, the one that the corporate staff had privately derided as a bunch of shade-tree mechanics had become engaged and capable of operating a world-class factory. The last plant manager cited these results:

- Quality parts per million defects fell from 1,500 to 3.
- Scrap loss reduction dropped from $3 million a year to $400,000.
- Overall equipment up-time rose to 92 percent.
- One typical part's price fell from $3.83 to $1.20 over five years.

> Charlie, the former UAW president and continuous improve-
> ment coach at the Tennessee plant credited for the turnaround
> to two successive plant managers, saying: "Changing our plant
> was 90 percent about good leadership." Yet Charlie was far too
> modest, because he himself best epitomized the ideal of being
> the change.

After nearly a decade of continuous improvement in the plant's facility,
equipment, processes, workforce skills, management's lean thinking, and
union member's buy-in to change, the factory's multinational owner decided
to depart the North American market for its products and sold it to another
multinational. After a few months, the new multinational announced that it
would move its contracts and machinery elsewhere and close the Tennessee
plant. They never gave employees an official reason for the closing. So on
a late summer afternoon, a final group of 140 said goodbye to their friends
and coworkers, trickled out to the parking lot, got in their cars, and left for
the last time.

There was no goodbye party.

Walking the shop floor among the idle machines on the last day, images
of my favorite union employees came to mind: Paul, who was always edgy
and challenging yet fun; Wormy, who always so honest and sincere; and
Charlie, the courageous union leader and continuous improvement coach.
My steps echoed as I walked over to the workstation where a female
employee had once described using a broomstick to dislodge jammed parts
for seven years. After that final day, Charlie used his severance pay to buy
equipment and now grinds stumps for a living in the county near the shuttered Tennessee plant.

Facing a challenging situation, two successive plant leaders had worked
long hours and six days a week for years. They had been mindful of work
processes on the shop floor, stayed present in the face of uncertainty and
conflict, and had turned the plant around. The North American division vice
president had shown great grit by investing to upgrade the plant facility and
equipment, even in the early years when it was unprofitable. The consultants flew in month after month and led kaizen and value stream mapping
events with great skill. Many union employees bought in, provided kaizen
ideas, and later sustained new lean work cells and lines.

When I drove out of the security gate for the last time that afternoon, I sensed the impermanence and imperfection of the modern corporate world and experienced a gut feeling that I couldn't put into words. The Japanese call this feeling, "mono no aware," meaning: "A sense of gentle sadness at the passing nature of all things, and an acute sensitivity to the tragic implications of even a single gesture."[2] Driving to the airport I reflected on my years working at the Tennessee plant and a startling personal realization arose. It was that in feeling that the plant was stuck in Ackoff's mess, I had been overly negative about the people, machinery, processes, and relationships that formed the plant's reality. The Japanese have a better term for it.

Wabi Sabi

Wabi Sabi is well-known sense of a deeper reality familiar to many Japanese people, yet its meaning can't be well articulated in words. Wabi is a term for an inner sense of the imperfect, irregular beauty things and of human beings in their natural state. Wabi is a perception that arises, for example, when contemplating the rough surfaces of weathered stones in a Zen garden, or witnessing a wrinkled smile on a happy senior citizen's face. Wabi has its roots in a mystical perception and a quiet appreciation of the root of things.

Sabi is a term for a lonely feeling that arises with the passage of time, an inner certainty that all life is impermanent. It can be sensed when touching a well-used hand tool, one discolored by generations of craftsmen, now gone. Author Andrew Juniper defines Wabi Sabi as: "An intuitive appreciation of a transient beauty in the physical world that reflects the irreversible flow of life in the spiritual world."[3]

Change leaders perceive the wabi sabi in an operation's aging facilities, in its used yet effective machinery, in its information technology and databases, in its processes and job descriptions, in its skilled employees, in its savvy supervisors, and in its apt technical experts – and they embrace the whole lot. They know that poor operational performance and defective products aren't "wrong," they are the natural consequence of everything that has gone before. And when an organization's leaders learn to stay present amidst it all, the problem of employee disengagement dissipates or dissolves completely. Transforming a business operation is a challenging journey, yet if you choose to learn the Sensei Way, you will become able to turn the five keys to a lean business transformation. However, even then, there's one big thing you'll have to do.

Notes

1 *Zen and the Art of Motorcycle Maintenance*, Harper Perennial Modern Classics, 2005, p. 117.
2 *A Traveler's Guide to the History of Japan*, Richard Tames, Interlink Books, 2008, p. 48.
3 *Wabi Sabi the Japanese Art of Impermanence*, Andrew Juniper, Tuttle, Publishing, 2003, p. 51.

Epilogue: Be the Change

Be the change that you wish to see in the world.[1]

Mahatma Gandhi

Not long after my years of lean coaching at the Tennessee plant came to a close, I accepted a three-week assignment to lead the redesign of the engineering change process in an aerospace factory. There, facing uncertainty and potential conflict with the plant's aggressive manager, and despite my years of experience, I once again had to realize and do the one big thing.

The plant's product was avionics boards which were destined for assembly into military aircraft. My project was to improve the speed and quality of the factory's engineering change notice (ECN) process. The ECN is a document commonly used in a factory to coordinate running technology upgrades among all relevant plant departments.

The plant manager was Jim, a 40-something millennial with an aggressive command-and-control management style. He often criticized factory employees to their faces, and he raged about low production and poor quality during his Friday morning staff meeting. When I arrived, Jim agreed to sponsor a 2-day lean event with his staff, a value stream mapping aimed to improve the ECN process. However, when I met with each of his staff members in private that first week, they felt that board production was far too chaotic to dedicate two full days to improving engineering change. Each believed that he had to be available to fight arising problems on the factory floor all of every day. So rather than complain to Jim, I embraced the wabi sabi, my feeling for the impermanent reality of an existing workplace. I agreed to interview each of them at their desks, map the current-state process on a table top, collect and assemble their improvement ideas, and draft future state of the ECN process for their review and further refinement the following week.

The rest of that first week I sat in each functional manager's office, listened and compiled his function's work in a "swim lane," his layer in the current-state map. As I let go of self-concern and gathered their ideas for improvement, I could see their resistance to me and the ECN project decrease. The second week, I circled back and reviewed a draft future-state map that I had complied from their ideas and adjusted it with their additional input. At the end of the third week, I was scheduled to deliver the future-state ECN value stream map plus a list of specific improvements to Jim at his Friday morning meeting.

Friday morning I did my usual mindfulness meditation before I left home. However, once on the road, rising concern obliterated my mindfulness. My mind played out various frightening scenarios about how Jim might reject my report and perhaps even belittle me in public, as I'd seen him do to others. I fanaticized witty come-backs to his imagined insults and at one point, even visualized punching him in the face. I was lost in my head, on the teeter-totter of anxiety and worry. Despite my morning meditation, I was a nervous wreck.

When I became aware of my state, I sat back in my car seat and began the presence kata. I took a series of deep breaths, found a rhythm, and became mindful of myself and my surroundings. I noticed tender, lime green spring leaves on the trees near the freeway. I sensed my bottom on the soft fabric of the seat, the fabric warmed by my body heat. I detected the imperfections in the road through the subtle vibrations of the steering wheel. I saw a flock of crows take flight from the field next to the highway.

At the next stop light, I observed the demeanor of the people sitting in the cars next to me. Some seemed anxious, their eyes darting around, while others appeared relaxed, perhaps listening to music. A few stared straight ahead, eyes glazed over, drivers who would soon present a risk to others on the road. Once rolling, I moved away from them.

Next, concentrating on the road ahead, I let go of self-concern and the state of presence arose in my consciousness. Then, right away, an insight struck me, and I silently asked myself: What am I actually afraid of? It's my last day of work at the avionics plant, so Jim can't fire me. Next I wondered: What real power does he have over me? My silent answer was that while he might complain to my consulting boss, I would simply tell him that, given the staff's limited availability, I'd done my best.

Then, with barely a pause, an intuition arose. It was that my overall life was going well. I had a comfortable home and a happy daughter going to high school, and despite periodic work frustrations, I was in good health and enjoying life. I liked my work leading kaizen events and mentoring managers on the Toyota Way. Driving again, a sense of peace arose inside me, and all my worries dissipated like that flock of crows I'd seen take flight from that field next to the freeway. My anxiety had been the result of listening to made-up stories in my own mind. The fact was, I didn't really know Jim well enough to predict how he would respond to my Friday presentation. Finally, I was struck by a profound revelation that arrived from beyond thought. It was that Jim couldn't disrupt my presence, because my state-of-being was fully within my own power. So I decided then and there that should Jim criticize me in the Friday staff meeting, I would stay present and that any critical comment would be, as a Zen saying goes: "Like a mosquito biting an iron bull."

I arrived at the plant a bit early, parked and went straight to Jim's conference room for the eight o'clock staff meeting. Taking my seat, I mindfully observed each staff member sitting in a cushioned chair around the table. Some appeared anxious, while others were staring out the windows, absent from the moment much as had been those dangerous drivers on the highway a few minutes before. Other staff members were intensely focused on their computer screens, eyebrows furrowed, perhaps rehearsing a powerpoint presentation or memorizing their data. Their goal, as it was each Friday, was to present their report and avoid being publicly humiliated by Jim during the meeting.

When Jim arrived, he began the meeting right away. Weekly updates started with the manager to Jim's immediate left, opposite my side of the table, and proceeded around one-by-one in order. Each manager spoke for five to ten minutes. By facing uncertainty and staying present I had dissolved a psychological wall that separated me from Jim, one I had built myself. Then, instead of an inner state of divorce, I silently bonded with him as a process improvement partner, albeit a volatile one.

Observing as others did their reports, another insight arose. It was that Jim was leading a chaotic factory, one that supplied avionics parts for military jets, and pilots' lives were at stake. Considering the staff members at the table, I recognized that he was really the only one standing between quality avionics boards and defective ones, mission-critical parts that could cause pilots to crash and die. At one point, I caught Jim's gaze, and we held eye contact for a brief moment. What I saw in his eyes in that moment wasn't anger and aggression, but an intense sense of purpose. Jim was plugging the quality gap for the whole factory in the only way he knew.

When I finally understood Jim's plight, I felt a wave of compassion for him. I decided then and there that should he criticize me during my presentation, I would stay present, show respect for the job he was doing, pass him my report and just say: I did my best. If his criticisms were warranted, I would revise or add to my report the following week on my own time. My response was neither cowardice nor the Stockholm syndrome.

It was the arising of altruism.

As the Friday meeting passed the halfway point, managers ever-closer to me delivered a report. When my turn to speak arrived, I hit the ground running and entered into flow. I mentioned the interviews and projected the future-state map for the ECN on the screen. I described and located each staff member's proposed changes, and included a couple of my own. A few of the proposed improvements were:

- Dividing the engineering change document into functional, semi-independent sections.
- Each manager having the ability to raise potential issues, even those outside their purview.
- Reducing the total number of signatures required by 25 percent.
- Empowering alternate managers to sign off on running changes when necessary.
- The engineering and production managers would share accountability for running changes.

As my presentation concluded, Jim's staff members rustled nervously in their comfortable conference room seats. They waited to see if I would get a pass from Jim or face withering criticism. Just as I made a final point my ten minutes were up, but Jim made no immediate comment. I slid the report across the conference room table as I had planned to do a few minutes before. He opened it, asked a couple of questions, seemed to understand my answers, and scheduled a follow-up meeting with two of his staff members. Then, a surprising thing happened.

Jim paused, turned his gaze back to me, nodded and smiled a bit, perhaps tipping his cap to my final pitch. Then holding a steely eye contact he said: Thanks for your work on this. Finished with me, he moved on to the staff member to my left.

Out in the hallway after the meeting, a friendly member of Jim's staff rushed up to me and breathlessly asked: What magic did you work on Jim? I've never seen him be so nice to a contractor, and you didn't even implement your project! I smiled, ignored his question, said thanks, shook his hand, and continued on my way out to my car. I walked away just as my first Japanese sensei had done decades before when I ask him a similar question.

I finally knew what he meant.

At the end of my quest I realized the way. Transforming a traditional business into a lean operation isn't devilishly difficult, nor are the vast majority of employees inherently resistant to change. People respond in kind to a change leader's state-of-being.

Namaste

Note

1 Gandhi Quotes on-line; attributed to Mahatma Gandhi; but this has historically been questioned.

Appendix 1: A Partial Retrospective on the Tennessee Plant's Lean Transformation with the Enneagram

The transformation of Tennessee plant's lean operations evolved over several years and achieved great gains in part cost, quality, delivery, and morale. At the time, I didn't know how to apply the Enneagram systems model to a lean transformation, but for illustration, below is a brief retrospective of a few highlights arranged around a few of its milestones. (Note that points seven, eight, and nine were never reached at the Tennessee plant due to subsequent events.)

At point one on the Enneagram of lean transformation, the corporate vice president mandated the implementation of Toyota-style lean operations at all the plants in his division. Ron, the new plant manager in Tennessee, had previously proven his management aptitude by turning around a smaller plant in the division, yet he had no experience implementing change in the Toyota Way. He had been a graduate of the General Motors Institute (now Kettering University) in mechanical engineering, and was a dedicated engineer and a very assertive manager. Growing up he had been a football linebacker in high school, and he still looked and acted the part. He commanded the respect of the plant's Southern employees, if not their affection.

Over the years, at the beginning of each monthly visit, I met with Ron in an executive coaching session for an hour or so to discuss CIP progress or project setbacks, and to reflect on what he was learning about his approach to leading change. One of his early reflections was: Everyone always knew where I stood. I would tell them how I really felt about each day's production or quality issues, usually without blaming individuals. Once I made the case that he needed to lead in a different way, he became open to reconsidering his leadership style. Over time he gradually changed his command and control approach to one more reasoned and participative. A couple of years later, he reflected differently saying: I'm trying to bring a new energy level and fresh eyes to the operation, plus get my staff to work together. I can pull them together and solve problems and I have seen some 'lights' come on.

Soon after I arrived, I facilitated a meeting with Ron's leadership team and the plant's union officials aiming to draft a joint vision. After I gave an orientation to lean production and led a visualization exercise in the meeting room, Ron and Bill, the union president, walked the shop floor. In walking and talking, they found a common purpose, that of achieving a world-class operation that would sustain the business and the plant's 400 good jobs. After the vision meeting, Ron told me: The most enlightening moment for me in the workshop was the idea of what a Best-In-Class facility would look like. It was insightful to see that both sides really did want a clean, well-run plant, and I became convinced that their work ethic would keep us going as an entity. Subsequently, Ron and Bill signed a letter of agreement to jointly sponsor a continuous improvement program, or "CIP." Since I lacked the Enneagram at that time, I didn't anticipate the milestone at point seven, "aligning leadership behaviors and management systems"; or tie milestone four, "value stream strategies and plans for developing people."

Soon after the visioning session, Ron hired a new operations manager, and he later recounted his initial day in the plant this way: When I began working at the Tennessee plant I thought I had walked back in a land of time. Grinding coolant was escaping CNC machine doors and spilling on the floor and on people. A mist of coolant filled the air, water was coming through the roof, and no one ever fixed anything. Indeed, it was to be a long journey from that state to a lean operation.

At milestone two on the Enneagram, a sensei or change leader mandates that all managers do a practice, immersion or experiment in order to change their basic thinking. Ron and the leadership team participated in an early 5S event, a couple of days when they all helped clean muck from under and around grinding machines. However, only a couple of his leadership team members ever joined a subsequent process kaizen events – most just checked in during the concluding presentations. Lacking the Enneagram, I did not anticipate the inner connection from milestone two to number eight, "identifying change leaders to develop others," nor did I look ahead to milestone four, tying key manager's immersion experience to "value stream strategies and plans for developing people."

According to the theory of the Enneagram, there will be disruptions in every change process at points three, six, and nine, and change leaders must intervene in order to resume progress. As an example at milestone three, "individuals who resist learning," one morning Bill stormed into Ron's office without an appointment. Perhaps due to internal union politics and despite his previous agreement to partner in the CIP program, he opened up on him. He said that it was bogus and that he would no longer allow his members to participate. Ron calmly stood up behind his desk, looked Bill in the eye, and said: That sign on the building just recently changed, and if that's your attitude, it'll be changing again soon. After a few face-saving comments, Bill left as abruptly as he came. In another point three incident, a shop employee walked up and challenged the operations manager saying: Rather than spend all this money improving the facility, why don't you just give us the money? He told the employee: I'm trying to improve the environment, bathrooms, locker rooms and make a nice clean place for you to work. The manager reflected later: Everybody thinks short term and I can't figure out why. In another illustrative incident at point three, he confronted a maintenance tech who claimed he had done a preventative maintenance assignment the previous day, but it was later discovered that he actually hadn't done it. The operations manager later recalled: I went up to him and asked him point blank, 'Why did you say this?' He stood quietly and gave no answer so I suspended him for three days." At milestone three, I did not anticipate the inner connections to number six, "identifying disruptions and value stream setbacks," nor did I connect from milestone three to nine, "(re)start lean learning and find a sensei" for a subsequent target area or facility.

At milestone four, "value stream maps and change plans" were completed for every production line and posted in the operations conference room. All production team meetings were held there, where teams reviewed metrics on production, cost, quality, and delivery, as well as discussing problems and follow-up on CIP projects. Visual management boards were established on all lines, and operations managers periodically did process confirmation on each line's constraint operation, calling in engineers and maintenance techs as needed. Since I lacked the Enneagram at that time, I did not consciously look back from milestone four to number one to align "current" progress with milestone one of "vision, strategy, and goals." Nor did I follow up during my visits to check if plant leadership team members were continuing to engage "a practice, immersion, or experiment"; which it turned out, they weren't.

At milestone five, "coaching and rapid improvement events in target areas," the lean consultants flew in to run kaizen events twice monthly, and they prepared Charlie, the CIP facilitator to run them in the future. In one event for example, a CIP team measured the process cycle times, quality defects, and downtime on their line. They presented Ron with data showing that the Petra, the machine central to production, could never consistently hold Toyota's tight part tolerance. Although there was no budget to replace it, he redirected existing funds and ordered a new machine the next day. This kind of personal commitment and corporate investment in the plant's future led many union members to buy in and participate in continuous improvement.

As the CIP program passed the three-year mark, a critical mass of managers, supervisors, and employees had bought into it. The CIP facilitator had been taught to lead improvement events. The plant manager and his operations leader spent many Saturday mornings brainstorming how to support improvement in the plant. Once returning on a plane from a benchmarking visit to a sister plant in Germany, they sketched a new vision on a napkin. It turned the plant's main lines by 90 degrees, shortening the flow across the narrow side of the plant's rectangle and in a line between incoming supply docks and the outgoing shipping docks. They later envisioned and built machining redundancy in those reoriented lines, making them more flexible for alternate production and thus more robust in the face of downtime or customer order changes. There was no corporate lean coaching model, other than the plan–do–check–adjust (PDCA) approach that had been taught during CIP events.

At milestone six, "value stream setbacks," the operations manager spent from two to four hours on the floor daily, checking production boards, auditing constraint operations, and assuring that maintenance techs followed up on CIP projects. When he engaged people on the shop floor, he was honest and factual. He remembered everyone's name and their prior commitments in detail. When some employees misrepresented production rates on a visual management board or denied responsibility for problems, he called them out. He later told me: Because I had been in machining so long, they couldn't bullshit me.

Some Tennessee workers carped that his management approach was too confrontational, called it a "Yankee" style of management, implying that it didn't fit the plant's Southern culture. He later said in private to me that: No one likes conflict, but it is necessary. My own view is that conflict is necessary and can be healthy, so long as it doesn't get personal. There is a fine line between assertive communication and destructive conflict, but when people begin name-calling, leaders must step in.

Several years into the Tennessee plant's journey to a lean business transformation, the operations manager told me: In the last two years, I have enjoyed coming to work, and now I can go away for a day or two and not worry about customers. We're not running any overtime, and we have 100 percent delivery performance.

Charlie, the continuous improvement coach, concluded at about that same time: Changing our plant was all about leadership. If you give it to them, people will participate.

Index

Note: **Bold** page numbers refer to tables, *Italic* page numbers refer to figures and page number followed by "n" refer to end notes.

Printed in the United States
by Baker & Taylor Publisher Services